D0496151

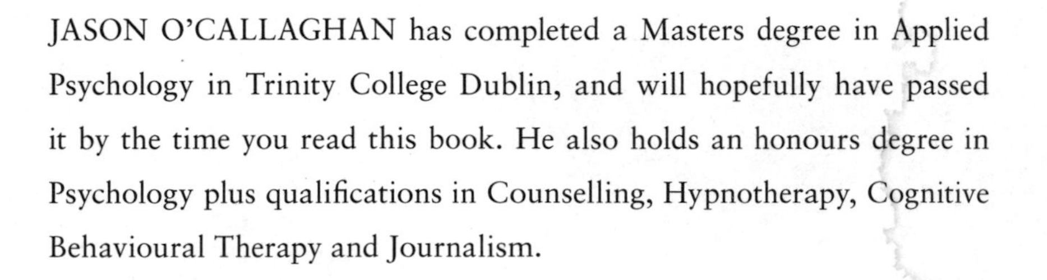

JASON O'CALLAGHAN has completed a Masters degree in Applied Psychology in Trinity College Dublin, and will hopefully have passed it by the time you read this book. He also holds an honours degree in Psychology plus qualifications in Counselling, Hypnotherapy, Cognitive Behavioural Therapy and Journalism.

For ten years he worked as a professional journalist for Independent Newspapers Ireland before retraining as a psychologist.

In 2012 he was named on the Trinity College Roll of Honour for his work in cancer research.

This is his second book. He is a director and therapist in The D4 Clinic in Dublin. www.D4Clinic.ie

GET THE LIFE YOU DESERVE

'29,000 DAYS'

WHAT WILL YOU DO WITH YOURS?

Jason O'Callaghan

© 2011 Jason O'Callaghan

Edited by Frank O'Beirne

The moral rights of the author has been asserted

All rights reserved

No part of the publication may be reproduced, stored in a retrieval system, or transmitted, in any form or by any means, without the prior permission in writing of the publisher, nor be otherwise circulated in any form of binding or cover other then that in which it is published and without a similar condition including this condition being imposed on the subsequent purchaser.

ISBNs

Parent: 978-0-9550889-1-9

ePub: 978-0-9550889-2-6

Mobi: 978-0-9550889-3-3

PDF: 978-0-9550889-4-0

A CIP catalogue for this book is available from the British library.

First published in Ireland in 2012 by The D4 Clinic

A D4 Clinic Product

www.D4Clinic.ie

Printed in Ireland by SPRINT-print Limited

For Carina and the bump

Contents

Foreword

By Ruth Field

(Best-Selling author of Run Fat Bitch Run)

29,000 days really brings home the fact that we don't have very long on this Earth and yet we are wasting days, months, years even being stuck in jobs we hate or in bodies we loathe or in relationships that are making us unhappy. We are not fulfilling our potential. At the crux of this second rate existence is our collective failure to take responsibility for our lives and our lacklustre attempts to change. Through a combination of visualisation techniques and inspiring stories of famous successful people whilst celebrating the incredible artistic ancestry of Ireland to inspire us, the author highlights the value of failure as a necessary stepping stone to success and the urgency with which we need to step up to the challenges in our own lives.

JASON O'CALLAGHAN is a man of ferocious energy and zeal and is a living example of the life he preaches in these pages. You will always have the life you have earned, no-one is going to hand it to you nor will it fall into your lap by chance. You have to go out and get it for yourself. And the clock is ticking. 29,000 days and counting..

'29,000 Days'. An Introduction

Congratulations on making the decision to change your life and to claim the life you deserve. Today will be the first time in your life when you are going to make 'no more excuses' for where you are in your life. It's time to take 100% responsibility for your own life. From this moment on things are going to be different.

If you want to lose weight, find love or get the job you have always wanted? If you want live the life that you have dreamed and reaching your potential, then join the ranks of the super-successful and get what you want out of live. The secrets of 29,000 days will help you get the life you deserve.

For over 4 years, I worked voluntarily within the psychological services in Ireland, obtaining an honours degree in psychology and a Masters in Applied Psychology from Trinity College, Dublin in my goal to learn the secrets on how to live the life that you have always wanted.

Using psychology and hypnotherapy research and practice I researched the secrets of positive living. My research revealed how humour can help cancer patients, how by taking 100% responsibility for your own life, you can release yourself from the shackles of your old life and give yourself the motivation and inspiration you need to fulfil your dreams.

This aim of this book is to help you realise that you can achieve your goals and you can set yourself on the road to achieving them.

No matter where you are in the world, no matter what your life situation is, this book can help you find the direction you need to have the life you deserve. Once you learn the secret of 29,000 days you will have an uncontrollable drive to get out in the world and get what life has waiting for you. Buying this book and reading it is just your first step. Remember that a journey of 1,000 miles starts with just one step.

From today on, it is time to take action and change your life. You are the only one who can do this. It's time to stop looking for others to hand it to you. It's time to stop being lazy and blaming other people for your situation. Once you do this, you will find a great weight lifted from your shoulders.

The world does not owe you a living or an easy life; remember the world was here first.

Anything you want in life, you will have to go out and get - make it happen. If something does not work out, try again. If that does not work out, try something else. From now on you will never give up or give in. You will make yourself be counted in this world. So from now on you will never feel sorry for yourself again. After all where has got you in the past? That's right, nowhere. So when something does not work, you will change it and try something that does work.

Let me tell you how this book is written. This book is written to motivate you. You will learn the secret of 29,000 days. This alone will be the greatest motivation you will ever get in your life. It's a simple secret but once it has hit home, you will not be able to stop yourself wanting to change right away.

This book will also tell you stories of those who have come before you. Not just famous people who have failed before they made a name for themselves in history. But, also stories from some people who were just normal and whose names you will never have heard before. You will read stories about how you possess something right now that they would give everything for.

You will read about the psychology of your own mind, why you are the way you are and why you have made choices you have made in the past. You will read about how no one in business wants you to be slim and healthy, because there is no money in it.

You will learn that size does not really matter and has nothing to do with success. You will read about how no matter what you wish to do in your life, someone else has done it before you and left you a map. How goal setting is the only way to achieve your dreams.

How the only good thing about having money is giving it away. How stress can kill you faster than junk food. How what number child you are in your family may affect your success in life.

How education can change the core of your personality. How to dismiss toxic people from your life. How smiling can help you live longer. How fear stops you living the life you deserve. How your perception can make you slim. How there are three different types of old age, two of which you really don't want to be. Why teenage brains really are different to the rest of the world. So if you are really ready for change, lets take this journey together.

Chapter 1

Is it time for a change?

Before I tell you the secret to what 29,000 days means, I want you to picture yourself standing in front of a mirror. When you look in the mirror, what do you see? Are you happy with the person looking back at you?

When you were younger, is this the person you thought you would turn out to be? Are you living the life you wished for? Do you remember when you were a child or even a teenager saying to friends: 'When I grow up, I am going to be a fireman, or a policeman, or an astronaut, or even a professional footballer.' Do you remember talking to friends in school and saying that you would love to have children, a career that satisfies your needs, a happy relationship, a happy home, a nice car, a chance to travel the world, to eat in nice restaurants? Ask yourself right now, are you living that life? If your answer is no, than ask yourself what happened?

Where is that person now, where have they gone and would you like to see them again? Would you like your days to be filled with excitement, challenges, money, happiness and love. Then the time has come to change. That time is not tomorrow, next week or next year. It is today. Today is your time to change.

This book is divided into a number of chapters, all of which deal with different issues. However, the overall goal of the book is simple. You get out of life what you put into it. If you want life to give you something, no matter how big or small that is, you must make a plan to get that and you must start today. This book is your guide to making that plan.

If you wanted to travel to a distant destination, you would plan your route, you would make your reservations, you would know how you were getting to the airport, your flight details, your hotel address, you would ensure that you had your medical shots before you left, that your passport was in date and that you had insurance and sufficient funds for your trip. In other words, you would plan ahead.

Life needs a plan to get you where you want to go. If you don't have this plan, how will you get there? Some people call it a map, a map to get where they want to be in life. This map can relate to any aspect of your life.

Let me explain with one simple example. If you are lonely and want to find a romantic partner, you can do things which will help you achieve this. You may first ask yourself, are you happy with how you look and how you talk, do you know what are you looking for in a relationship and would you know it if you found it?

Are you confident talking to people of the opposite sex? Are you able to chat to someone that you find attractive? If you answered 'no' to any of these questions, then maybe you need to start with improving yourself before heading out on your first date. This may involve you first making a list of these improvements in yourself that you need to change first.

However, if you are happy with yourself, we move onto the next step. How we get to meet the right person. We live in a wonderful age, the internet means that now we don't even have to leave the comfort of our own house to meet the person of our dreams. In the US, the majority of dating now starts online. It's cheap and safe and allows you to dip your toe in the water without having to worry about making a quick exit. You will meet some people you like and some you don't like. You will meet some who like you and some who don't. It's an adventure and that is the fun. Just like life, it's an adventure. This is an example of the map I mentioned. A map for finding a partner or even better the love of your life. You have no way of knowing what lies ahead until you try.

The Future is promised to no-one

If we knew everything which lay ahead of us from one day to the next, some of us would never get out of bed in the morning. If I told you now that I could tell you the date you would die, would you want to know?

On the one hand, you could plan everything you wanted to do for every day until then, getting to see everyone, getting to experience everything you wanted to, maybe completing your bucket list, (that list of things you said you always wanted to do before you died).

However, no one can tell us the date we are going to die. So, every day we wake up, we should say to ourselves one thing. We should say 'Thank you for giving me another day, now what am I going to do with it?'

During my training as a psychologist, I specialised in psychooncology, which is the psychological treatment of cancer patients, their families and carers. Some of these patients survived and overcome cancer. Sadly, some did not.

There is one thing that each of those cancer patients who did not make it, would give anything to have what you have today, and that is the gift of life. Just one more day to watch the sunrise, to sit on a beach, to play with their children or grandchildren, to chat to a loved one, to kiss their partner, to eat a wonderful meal with friends, to laugh aloud, to travel, to go for a nice walk in the sun, to help others less fortunate than themselves. All these things that these people can no longer do, you can do right now, this very minute.

I once worked with an old barman who made a comment to me which would change my life. He had worked for several years in Australia and had come home to Ireland to go into semi-retirement, working part time in a hotel. He said to me: 'Son, remember to treat every day like it is your last, because one day you will be right'. It's something that I think about every day.

The following day, I applied to college as a mature student to study journalism; that one comment changed the direction of my life and it can also lead to the decision which changes your life.

Just one more day

What would you do if you only had one more day to live? A famous writer once said that some people are so busy making a living that they forget to live. In my clinic I come across this every day, either with men, who work all the time and then spend no time at home with their wife or kids. They get stressed, spending their lives working and commuting to work. Then, by the time they get home, they don't have time to play with the kids or to chat with their wife. One day they come home and the house is empty - the wife and the kids have left.

Women can spend so much time taking care of everyone else around them, from their parents, to the in-laws, to kids, to their husband, that they then put on weight from not eating correctly and not exercising enough. They may then fail to look after their hair or skin, never shopping for themselves. They gain weight, start to lose their confidence, get depressed about their body and looks, eventually in some cases becoming ill from the negative effects of stress.

In the clinic I always start by asking these ladies if they have ever been on a commercial flight. Most people have of course been on a plane. So I say do you ever notice that the stewards always tell parents travelling with children that if the oxygen masks are dropped down in case of emergency, they should put on their own mask first, before attending to their children.

This is because you will be no use to the child if you can't breathe yourself. It's like that in life too. What is the use in rushing around doing so much that you make yourself ill, stressed and depressed? You are trying to keep all the balls in the air, doing everything yourself, and as a result you may not be around to be with the people you are helping every day.

While working with groups of cancer patients I often talk to them about the dangers of stress, which is commonly known as the silent killer. In every group, there are patients who put their hand up even before I finish speaking and say: 'Stress is what gave me cancer.' Some claim it is stress in relation to work, some with relationships issues, some with problems relating to money, family or children.

We don't know from a medical point of view what mix of causes results in someone getting cancer. However, we do know that smoking, a bad diet, a lack of exercise, stress and sometimes genetics can contribute to a cancer diagnosis. We are sure that chemicals such as those found in cigarettes cause 90% of lung cancer cases. So if you are a smoker, I suggest you stop today.

What would you do for free?

The first question I would like you to ask yourself is: 'what job would I do for free'? What job would you do without being paid? Would it be to sing, to play a sport, to write, to travel or to help others who are less fortunate than you?

It does not matter what it is, but it is your first step in gaining the secret of 29,000 days. So please, right now, get a blank sheet of paper and write on it what would your dream life be. This can relate to your body, your work, relationships, family, car, house, kids: it really does not matter, it is just for you to keep as personal and private as you want.

Now what I want you to do is place your left finger and thumb together. As you do this, see yourself in your mind standing in front of the mirror you stood in front of during the first line of this chapter.

Or even better make it a gold leafed beautiful mirror. Now see yourself looking the way you want to look once your dream life is complete. You may have lost weight or changed your hairstyle and your clothes. How do you look now as you look in that mirror? Look at what you are wearing, how slim, tanned and healthy you look.

The love of your life may be with you, maybe you are in the uniform of your dream job, maybe you are dressed in a smart business suit. Maybe behind you is the place you wish to live, the stunning house, the beach resort you are staying in. It really does not matter what you see once it is how you want to be in the future, the person you want to be and the person you can be.

Now every time you need to reinforce your goals, your drive and your ambition, press your left hand finger and thumb together as hard as you can and see yourself again standing in front of that mirror. Look at every detail of what you are wearing, in more detail each time - notice your hair, your make up (if you are a woman), your shoes, the detail in your clothes, notice what and who is in the mirror with you.

Now look at the expression on your face. What would you call that? Confidence, happiness, contentment? You can feel the hairs standing up on the back of your neck, because you know this is what the future holds for you.

Jack Canfield, who wrote the best-selling book, 'How to get from where you are to where you want to be', said that you must take 100% responsibility for your life and I agree. To start your journey to change, to start understanding what 29,000 days means, this is the first challenge you must face.

Today, if you are unhappy, this sadly is your fault. If you are not in the job you want, the relationship you want, if you do not have the car you want, the house you want, the body you want. It is not my fault, your partner's fault, the kids' fault, your parents' fault, your friends' fault, your schoolteachers' fault, your boss's fault or even the Government's fault. It is your fault and it is down to you, once you accept this fact it will allow you to change.

This is a big responsibility to deal with. But, take it from me, once you accept that only you can take control of your life, it will feel like a giant weight has been lifted off your shoulders.

Once you accept full responsibility for your life, from that minute on, things will start to change. Once you do this and say to yourself: 'I am where I am in life because of decisions I have made and choices I have made in my life', you are already 50% of the way to becoming the person you deserve to be and having the life you deserve to have.

You must accept that it was you who ate the junk food, left school early, married the wrong person, didn't bother to exercise, didn't retrain after you lost your job, did not sign up to a college course, didn't save for a rainy day, bought the wrong house in the wrong area, spent everything you earned trying to keep up with others who earned more than you. If you accept that no one put a gun to your head to make these choices, that it is you alone that can change your future, then you can change your life. We all have choices.

In his autobiography, Richard Branson says that amazing things happen when you say yes. Just imagine for a moment that you said yes to every opportunity - not silly things which would put yourself or your family at risk - but simple everyday choices.

I try to say yes to as many things as I can. When I say yes, I open my comfort zone. The comfort zone can be defined as 'what we are comfortable doing or not doing.' The thing about the comfort zone is that it is either expanding or shrinking. It never stays the same.

So once we say 'yes', we are making our comfort zone bigger and opening our world up to more experiences and opportunities. Once we say 'no', we are closing out new experiences and opportunities.

I learnt this lesson myself in 1992, when as I had a summer job in Paris working in Disneyland as a waiter. One night, myself and some of the other staff met a man in our restaurant who was married to and managed La Toya Jackson, the sister of the late Michael Jackson. She was performing in the world famous Moulin Rouge in the centre of Paris. He invited a few us to the show and for dinner.

Now, we lived next to Disneyland which was an hour by train to Paris and getting home in the early hours of the morning to Disneyland was near impossible and would mean having to wait until morning to get the 6am train. So, when everyone else said yes and went, I said no and stayed home alone. When the others arrived at the door, their tickets were waiting for them, they had the best table in the house, with free dinner and champagne and after the show, a car was waiting to bring them home. Lesson learnt.

As the famous saying goes, when life gives you lemons, make lemonade. Sometimes things will work out, sometimes they don't, but in my experience there is no such thing as failure - Just education.

Say for example you are reading this and saying to yourself: 'I am miserable in my job, I hate getting up every morning to make the commute to work, I am underpaid and I hate my boss'.

This of course is a very common thing for someone to say. However, you now have two choices - you can stay in the job for the rest of your life or you can leave. You of course will say to me: 'if I leave, which I really want to, who will pay my rent, who will put food on the table'?

I am not saying you need to leave your job today, what I am saying is that you are the only person who can change your future. Therefore, first you must admit that you are the one who took the job. Therefore you can also get another job. This may mean staying in your current job for a few more months or even a year. But, at least you now have a plan. As I have mentioned earlier in this chapter, the first thing you are going to do is make a plan and write it down now.

Write down the job you want, once it is realistic. There is little point writing down that you want to be a world class footballer if you are 65 years old. Pick a goal that is realistic and a job which you have as much a chance of doing as anyone else. Then plan the route to getting that job.

That job may even be working for yourself. So start with making that plan. Does it require you to go back to school, college or university? How will you fund this? Will you have to do a night job if you study during the day? Where can you get experience for your new career? Can you work for free during the day for a company within the field, while working in the evening to support yourself? It does not matter what the job or career is, all that matters is that you sit down and plan the journey.

In Japan, they say that a journey of 1,000 miles starts with a single step. This is your journey, that piece of blank paper in front of you is the first step, this will be followed by the second step, the third step and so on - until you are the person you want to be. That person you see in the mirror when you press your left hand finger and thumb together.

Remember from now on that other people's opinion of you is none of your business, you do not care what anyone else has to say about you or what they think; you will always take good advice, but remember that from now on it is your view which matters. Others will think you are mad, crazy, too spontaneous, not realistic. Let them think that - in fact, don't even tell them what you are planning until you are well along the road to doing it. Remember that 'he who says something can't be done is normally interrupted by someone else doing it'. People who succeed in life play their cards very close to their chests, revealing their plans only when they are close to fruition.

For ten years I interviewed celebrities, world leaders and

businessmen, and all the ones I remember said little and listened a lot. So keep your plans to yourself. It has to be your dream, your plan, your new direction in life. Because you are the only one that matters in this equation. Concentrate on your views, your time, your effort and in return you will get your results.

This is your dream life, so few people will understand where you are coming from. Few will see things from your perspective, few will have your drive. It's important at this stage to introduce the 80/20 rule. This rule is pretty much universal and its very simply.

80% of people work for the other 20%. 80% of people drive the car they have to drive, 20% drive the car they want to drive. 80% of people are in the job they have to do, 20% in the job they want to do. You can apply the 80/20 rule to nearly every aspect of life. So as you read these words you need to ask yourself one question before you move onto the next chapter; 'do I want to stay in the 80% or am I ready to move into the 20%'?

Others who have come before you in the journey include nearly every Hollywood actor and actress, every best-selling author, every world famous sports star, Oscar winning film director, every record breaking musician and singer, every well known chat show host, every astronaut, every American President, every world leader and Prime Minster, every CEO of a global business, every inventor from Thomas Edison to James Dyson. They have all overcome the odds to rise to the top of their chosen profession.

James Dyson is the man who reinvented the vacuum cleaner and is now worth £1.5 billion. In the 1980's, Dyson was forced to set up his own production company for his new invention as none of the bigger companies would help him make it. Dyson tells the story of how during his school days he was a good long distance runner, saying: 'I was quite good at it, not because I was physically good, but because I had more determination. I learnt determination from it'. These words should give you a warm feeling inside. Determination is the key to success. If you fall down seven times, than get up eight times.

As we start this journey to change, you need to remember that nothing happens without action. The Grammy Award winning comedian Jonathan Winters said: 'If your ship doesn't come in, then swim out to meet it'. From now on everything you do and say will relate to your new goals.

Start with using the present tense. Say 'I am' - these words are positive, present and affirmative. Keep your goals to the point and short. Your goals should be once sentence, like 'I am going to earn $/£100,000 within one year.' Or 'I am going to find a new job that I really love within six months'. Make it specific to yourself, this is your goal, your aim, the change you are going to make in your life. If it is to get a new slimmer body, than say; 'In six months I will have lost ____ pounds/ kilograms'. Than get ready to move onto the next step.

Once we have the goal fixed, the time scale agreed and the plan made, your next step is to ask yourself, are you willing to make this your obsession. It will require hard work and long days, and dedication to your dream but remember the great words of Yoda in Star Wars, 'There is not try, there is only do.'

We only do

From now on, we only do. We do not say 'I am going to try to lose weight', we say 'I am going to lose weight'.

We do not say I am going to *try* to find the job of my dreams or try to find the man/ woman of my dreams. We say I am *going to* find the job or the man/ woman of my dreams. No more trying, just doing. You have been trying for years. Now, it's time to do.

So what is 29,000 days and how will it change your life?

To explain what 29,000 days is, I want to you do a simple mathematical calculation. I want you to ask yourself a question - in your life from the time you are born until the time you die, how many days are you on the planet?

In other words how many days are you alive. This requires you to look at people's average life span. The current US statistics state that an average person (man or woman) will live until they are about 80 years old (79.5 to be exact.)

So let's take it as 80 years of age. That is 80 years multiplied by 365 days to get the average amount of days we are alive, that's 29,200 (29,000 to make it easier for you to remember) from the day we are born until the day we die (on average). Some of us will live a little longer, some shorter. No matter who you are, from Frank Sinatra to the Pope. No matter how much money you have or how famous you become. That's it, the show is over and the curtain will come down.

So if you are currently 60 years old, you have already used 21,900 days, leaving you with 8,000 or so days left. If you are 40 years old, you have used 14,600 days, leaving you with 15,000 days left and if you are only 20 years old, 7,300 days are already gone, leaving you with only 21,000 or so days left.

Once we put it like that, it really puts things into perspective. That figure of 29,000 days is it. When I reveal this to clients in my clinic or at conferences, some people get depressed. I explain in detail that 29,000 days is it, that's life. That's the whole shooting match, that's the final whistle. That's when there really are no more tomorrows.

Those who have ended up in Alcoholic Anonymous or other ten or twenty steps programmes have a motto to define insanity. It's doing the same thing over again, but expecting a different result.

If you keep doing the same thing you always do, you will get the same results you always got. If you continue to eat junk food, do not save, do not take time to exercise, ignore your partner and kids, do not service your car, do not plan for the future or write down your ambitions, do not dream to dream and act on your wishes. Then you will get the same results you have always got.

If you fail to write down where you are going, how you are going to get there and what you are going to do once you get there, than you will get the same results you have always got and you will end up in the same position you have always ended up in.

So, ask yourself honestly if it is time for a change, once and for all.

Stop thinking, talking, promising, putting off until tomorrow, stop ignoring that feeling that life has something better in store for you.

Someday there will be no tomorrow.

Tomorrow is promised to no-one. Time waits for no person, those days are clocking down, one by one. How many have you got left, do the calculations right now, multiply your age today by 365, then subtract this number from 29,000. That's if you're lucky enough to make it to 80 years of age. Do you have the number now, the number of days you have left until the show is over and the curtain comes down?

Write it down here. On average, I have ___________________ days left.

So the final question is 'what are you going to do with these days?' No more putting off until tomorrow what you can do today.

If your number was 20,000 days left, than tomorrow it will be 19,999, the next day it will be 19,998 days, the clock just keeps ticking down.

It's time to take action, it's time to make that list, it's time to pick up the phone or click on the mouse, it's time to sign up to that course or to start to exercise. Whatever you want to do, today is the day to start.

Now more than ever, it's time to find that direction that you have been looking for. It's time to stop re-creating the wrong life for yourself over and over again. No one else can do it for you. No more excuses, no more psychological escape hatches, such as 'I could do this - but'. That all stops today.

From today you are taking full responsibility for your own life. Remember if it was easy everyone would be doing it. You goal must challenge you, but it has to be measurable - a set time, a set figure, a set weight, a set reward. It does not matter what it is but make it worth fighting for.

Don't worry if you get down or tired of trying. Nothing worthwhile ever came easily. Just think about the first time you tied your own shoe laces - it was difficult. The first time you rode a bike - it was not easy. The first exam you passed, the first medal you won in school, the first girl/ boy you kissed. The first job you got, the first house you bought, the first loan you got. It was never easy but you did it.

So it will be hard at times but it will also be much easier than you ever imagined and the final results will make every one of those days on your countdown clock better than you ever could have dreamt.

So get ready to jump, we don't wait until we have wings, we jump and build our wings on the way down. So let's jump!

Chapter 2

P+R=R

'You only live once, but if you do it right, once is enough' (Mae West)

Everything from now on is a challenge to you, but this is a good thing. Because from today, you will look at life differently. The reason you will do this is that you now know that the clock is ticking. Today is another day that will be taken from your 29,000 days. So what are you going to do with today?

Oscar Wilde, the great Irish poet and playwright said 'To live is the rarest thing in the world, most people exist, that's all.' From today, your life of existence is over.

Will you take up a new challenge today? Continue with the first steps on your list? Remember, no matter what happens today, life goes on, no matter what you have learnt so far, today is a new day. Today and from now on, you are going to look at problems in a different way.

To obtain the life you want, you need to look at the world around you and how you deal with issues that come up on a daily basis. This involves the P+R=R formula. This formula can be adapted to fit everything in your life - every problem, every relationship, every situation, every activity, every confrontation, your relationship with your friends and family, your boss and work colleagues.

P+R=R means: 'Problem plus reaction equals result'. The

significance of every problem from now on will only be determined by your reaction to it.

Why do some people get emotional if something does not go their way? Why do some people stress over everything, while others just let things pass them by? Why do some people spend every minute worrying about money while others never care? Why do some people spend their lives thinking about what people think of what they do and what they look like, while others could not care less?

It is all related to the reaction to a problem, situation, issue or activity. The damaging thing is not the problem or the issue, but the reaction to it. So before you react to anything or anyone, stop and think about your reaction. Is it really worth your time and energy?

Here are some simple things you can change today to help you improve your reaction to issues which may come up. Remember it's your reaction to the problem or person which will determine the result of the situation.

- Give up your need to always be right, let your ego go. Life is too short.
- Give up your need for control, be yourself and let others be themselves.
- Give up blaming others for your problems: it's your fault, so accept it. If someone did something to you, just learn from it. Remember the old saying: 'Fool me once, shame on you, fool me twice, shame on me'.
- Give up on self-defeating talk. You have plans and things to do

now, so you can't afford the luxury of a negative thought.

- Give up on limiting beliefs; stop thinking what you can or can't do, just do it.
- Give up complaining; no one cares.
- Give up the luxury of criticism of people and things. Life is too short, just let it be.
- Give up the need to impress others. No one is thinking about you and no one cares as they are all too busy living their own lives so just do what makes you happy. Contentment and happiness cannot be bought or found with fame.
- Give up your resistance to change; change is good.
- Give up on judging people. Live and let live, no matter what religion, sexual orientation or place someone is from. Remember that your mind will only work once it is open.
- Give up on your fears. Don't fail to act because you are afraid to fail. Mistakes are just opportunities for learning something new.
- Give up on your excuses. Aim and fire. Some people spend their lives talking about changing, but they never do anything about it. They spend their lives aiming but failing to shoot. Take the shot. Remember the days are counting down.
- Give up the past, it's gone. Look in front of you now, that is your future and that is all that really matters.
- Give up living your life to other people's expectations. Live your life for yourself, remember that life is not a dress rehearsal; this is it, the days are counting down. Make each one count. I will go into a more detailed version of the above in Chapter 5.

Progress will always involve risk and you must leave the shade of the family tree to bask in the sunshine. Goals require change and change requires taking chances. How you do anything is how you do everything so if you are going to do something from now on, do it 100%. Don't be afraid, because fear is not real. Getting the feeling that something terrible is going to happening means that it has not happened yet and most likely will not happen at all. Mark Twain once said 'I have lived a long live and had many troubles, most of which never happened.'

You don't need permission to live the life you want from now on, you have a right to it. Authority is 20% given but 80% taken. So take it today. From now on you do not have time to be fearful, to be guilty, to feel unworthy, to have hurt feelings, to be discouraged, to make excuses. You must wake up if you wish to live your dreams. You need to challenge that comfort zone, to shake the tree which is your life and wake it up. You will need to change habits, moving from negative habits to positive ones.

Each one of us is a cocktail made up from the day we are born. Into this cocktail comes what we learn from our parents, our families, our friends, our education, the place we live in, the place we go to school and our place in the family. Did you know that nearly half of all American Presidents were the first born or only children? Look at Jimmy Carter, George W. Bush, Lyndon Johnson, all first born. Did you also know that the majority of US Astronauts were also first born or only children?

Everything that you are and everything that you have done in your life has been learnt. In psychology we call it 'modelling.' We learn from watching those around us. Queen Elizabeth II said it best: 'I learnt like monkey learns, from watching its parents'. So that fear that you feel, that limiting power that stops you doing things that others do is something that you have learnt over the years. It may be from parents or through school, it may be from TV or friends. But, just as you learnt this, you can also unlearn it. It is just a habit and now it is time to change that habit.

The first word you need to remove from your vocabulary from now on is the word 'but'. This little three letter word is the main psychological escape hatch password. For example people often start with the statement; 'I am going to lose weight BUT I am too busy with work' or 'I am going to get a new job BUT I am going to wait until the New Year to do it' or 'I want to break up with my abusive husband BUT I am staying with him for the sake of the kids'. Whatever the issue in your life, the word BUT always gets in the way of change.

The truth is that if you wanted to lose weight, get a new job or leave your abusive husband, you could. Thousands of people change everyday. Are you just too afraid or too lazy? I know that sounds harsh, but it could also be true.

Losing weight would mean paying attention to your diet and exercising more. This would involve change and work, so it's easier to claim that you want to change but that you don't have time to buy and cook healthy food, you don't have time to get to the gym or attend a class, you don't have time for a walk or a run. Leaving your job to find one you are really happy in would mean that you may have to retrain, return to college, do interviews, meet new people, travel a different route, maybe start on a slightly smaller salary.

I'm sure you could give yourself a lot of reasons not to bother. So instead you sit there every day, complaining to your co-workers about how you hate your job, complaining to your partner about your boss. Yet day in and day out, you do nothing about it but you keep talking about leaving BUT you never do anything about it. Yet again, as every day goes by, think of the 29,000 days. How many days have you wasted in a job you hate? 1,000, 2,000, 10,000?

In life there are two types of people - people who make excuses and people who get results. Those who make excuses also constantly blame others for their problems and complain about their lives. Those who get results accept that this is their life and that they are responsible for it. Like the great modern author J. K. Rowling, they understand that 'it does not do to dwell on dreams and forget to live.'

Life is for living, you need to get your plan together and get moving today. The days are ticking down. Plan and execute, aim and fire. This is your time to change. One of the greatest people to grace this planet was the late Mother Teresa. She was once quoted as saying the following about life:

'Life is an opportunity, benefit from it. Life is beauty, admire it. Life is a dream, realise it. Life is a challenge, meet it. Life is a duty, complete it. Life is a game, play it. Life is promise, fulfil it. Life is sorrow, overcome it. Life is a song, sing it. Life is a struggle, accept it. Life is a tragedy, confront it. Life is an adventure, dare it. Life is luck, make it. Life is too precious, do not destroy it. Life is life, fight for it'.

In order not to waste another day, you must open your mind fully. This will involve treating everyone you meet from now on the same way – everyone from the garbage man to the President. Make no more assumptions about types of people, who they are or where they are from. To change yourself must mean that you have an open mind not just about your environment but also about yourself and others.

Visualisations are how we create the world as we want it to be, just as we did in Chapter 1, when I asked you to see yourself in the mirror as you wish to look, than pressing your left hand finger and thumb together. I now want you to reinforce this by doing it again. See the mirror and see your image in it, press your left finger and thumb together again, see yourself in front of that mirror, look at the image again, notice more about what you are wearing, every detail about the image, the expression on your face, who is with you in the image, how tanned and toned you look.

From today on you are simply taking steps towards that image, every day is a step closer to the person that you want to be. If the new you is slimmer and your goal is to lose weight, every time you exercise and listen to your body when you eat, eating little and often, eating only when you are hungry, you are than taking a step closer to the new you, the one in the mirror you can see each time you press your left hand finger and thumb together.

However, if you come up with excuses – BUTS - for why you can't find time for your daily exercise, or you don't take time to eat the right type of food in smaller portions, all you are doing is taking a step away from that image. It's that simple.

If your goal is to get a dream career and today you applied for a new job, updated your resume, went online to look up new positions, again you are taking a step closer to that image of the new you in the mirror. Maybe in the image you are wearing a business suit, looking smart and excited about another great day in a job that you love.

However, if you got up, went to your old job, complained all day, said to yourself while sitting in your cubicle or office: 'I hate this building, I hate my boss, I hate this job' and you did nothing about it, then nothing will change.

If you do the same thing every day, you will get the same results every day. If you are unemployed and you stayed in bed late today, got up and watched terrible day time TV, played video games or watched movies all day, you have failed to do anything towards getting a new job. You won't get one by doing this every day.

Get the plan in place and put the plan for your new life in action. In my clinic, the most common treatment I do is gastric band hypnotherapy. This involves hypnotising clients into believing that have had a gastric band fitted to curb their eating habits.

I make the operation real, by playing hospital sounds, such as heart monitors and ventilators. I swab the clients' hands with TCP, to give a surgical smell. I also put a spotlight above their heads. All this makes them feel that they are really in the operating theatre.

You need to make your new life a reality by starting with the things you can control. As much as possible you should dress well, look well and talk well. Print images of the clothes you are going to wear once you have lost the weight. If you already have clothes you want to fit into, hang them on the outside of your refrigerator. This will remind you every time you go to eat that you are really determined to lose weight.

Get images of the car you want to drive when you have your new job. Get a picture of the house you want to live in once you have the money you desire. Keep it as a screensaver on your computer. Make your future a reality little by little by changing the little things you can change while you are waiting for the big changes to happen. Some of my clients write their goals down in a book, or on a chart or a vision board. A vision board is something you can put on your wall and add to it anything that helps to remind you of your dream life. This can be houses, cars, clothes, jewellery, winning an Oscar. It does not matter, this is your vision board. Keep it private if you prefer by putting the article or images in a book and adding to it daily.

The secret of the Irish

Size does not matter. No matter what you come up with as an excuse for not doing something you should never claim it is who you are or where you are from. Over the years I have interviewed a lot of famous people. Some have been great and nice to work with, some inspire, some don't. Some come from a wealthy background, but the majority come from middle class or working class backgrounds. Yes, they have all made it to be world famous and have millions of pounds or dollars in the bank.

This reminded me of something which has always jumped out at me about the small country I come from - Ireland. We live on a small island on the west coast of Europe and from a list of 242 countries in the world we are only the 119th biggest, with a population of around 4.5 million people - between Norway and the Central African Republic.

Now let's look at some of the other countries. Turkmenistan has a bigger population (5.2m) than Ireland but how many famous and successful people have you heard from who have come out of Turkmenistan? How many of you reading this have even heard of Turkmenistan or could point it out on the map?

China has the biggest population in the world, followed by India. Together, they have a population of over 2.5 billion people. The USA only has a population of just over 314 million people, followed by Indonesia with 237 million people.

So Ireland only has 4.5 million people. If you are reading this in the Europe that is little more than the population of Berlin alone. If you are reading this in the USA, it is similar to the population of Los Angeles and in Australia, similar to Sydney.

So our tiny island, on the western fringes of Europe has only 4.5 million people, yet we have some of the world's biggest rock bands such as U2, Van Morrison, Thin Lizzy, The Pogues, The Cranberries, The Script, The Chieftains, Enya, boy bands such as Westlife and Oscar winning musicians such as Glen Hansard, whose song from the movie 'Once' won best soundtrack and is now a part of the hit show on Broadway.

We have also produced one of the world's biggest theatre shows - Riverdance. Some of the world greatest actors come from Ireland, including Pierce Brosnan, Kenneth Branagh, Gabriel Byrne, Michael Fassbender, Fionnuala Flanagan, Oscar Winner Brenda Fricker, Richard Harris, Liam Neeson, Oscar Winner Peter O'Toole, Maureen O'Hara, Saoirse Ronan and Colin Farrell. Even double Oscar winner Daniel Day-Lewis has adopted Irish citizenship as has the dancer Michael Flatley. Oscar winning directors Neil Jordan and Oscar nominated director Jim Sheridan are also Irish.

Authors such as Bram Stoker, who wrote Dracula, was Irish as was Maeve Binchy. Other famous Irish writers include John Banville, Brian Friel, Nobel Laureate Seamus Heaney, James Joyce, Patrick Kavanagh, Sean O'Casey, John Millington Synge, Oscar Wilde and William Butler Yeats.

All this talent from a country the size of Los Angeles. Think about this the next time you come up with any type of excuse as to why you can't do something, why you can't go somewhere, why you can't change your own life because of who you are, where you come from, who your family is or how much education you have had. Just remember it's not the size of your country or city that matters, it is who you are that matters.

Ask the right person at the right time

A lot of clients call to my clinic and complain about issues in their lives. They tell me about someone who did something to them – maybe their partner or their boss. It can be one of a hundred different issues. Some are more complex than others. However, sometimes I ask them whether they have talked to the person in question about the issue they are having. The normal response is 'Oh no, I can't'. Then I ask why?

It's normally fear - fear of being fired, fear of rejection, fear of upsetting the other person's feelings. I ask them if they would prefer to be upset rather than upset the other person? The answer seems to be 'Yes', which is generous, but not very helpful to the client.

This other person is doing something to offend, upset or insult you but you are so worried about upsetting them, that you would rather be upset than confront them. I know it's hard to understand when it is put to you like that but this is what we have all done at one time or another.

You know the feeling of butterflies in your stomach, that release of adrenaline you get when you know you have to do something, to resolve something, to ask for a pay rise or a day off work. No matter how small or big the issue is, why do we get this feeling? The adrenaline comes from fear and a condition that psychologists call the 'flight or fight response'. Most people do not know that it is actually called the 'flight, fight or freeze response', as some birds like pigeons go into a frozen state when faced with danger, so the predator thinks they are already dead.

When we experience excessive stress, whether from internal worry or external circumstances, such as a dangerous situation, the bodily reaction is triggered. This was originally discovered by the great Harvard physiologist Walter Cannon; he called this response a function that is hard-wired into our brains and that represents a genetic wisdom designed to protect us from bodily harm.

This response corresponds to an area of our brain called the hypothalamus, which, when stimulated, initiates a sequence of nerve cell firing and chemical release that prepares our body for running or fighting.

The flight or fight response comes from pre-historic days when man was out hunting in the dessert of sub Saharan Africa and he came across a tiger. He had few choices, he could out run the tiger or he could stay and fight it. Either way one of them was not going home for dinner. So the body kicks in with a lot of biological responses to this stressful situation.

When our fight or flight response is activated, sequences of nerve cell firing occur and chemicals like adrenaline (epinephrine), noradrenaline and cortisol are released into our bloodstream. These patterns of nerve cell firing and chemical release cause our body to undergo a series of very dramatic changes. Our respiratory rate increases. Blood is shunted away from our digestive tract and directed into our muscles and limbs, which require extra energy and fuel for running and fighting. Our pupils dilate. Our awareness intensifies. Our sight sharpens. Our impulses quicken. Our perception of pain diminishes. Our immune system mobilises with increased activation.

We become prepared - physically and psychologically - for fight or flight. We scan and search our environment, 'looking for the enemy.'

However, fights between man and tigers are very rare in modern society. But, the body still goes into this fight or flight sequence when we are stressed. This may be in the office, at home, on the phone, in the car due to traffic. The stress may be due to money worries, family worries, the constant stream of 24 hour media or constant social media interaction and the modern world we live in. Each time we get stressed, we release chemicals but unlike in the past now we are not burning these chemicals off by fighting or running, we are just becoming more and more stressed.

This is turn blocks up our arteries and this in time will cause high blood pressure, then heart attacks and strokes. High stress has also been found over time to have links to cancer. The evidence is overwhelming that there is a cumulative build up of stress hormones. If these hormones are not properly metabolised over time, the resultant excessive stress can lead to disorders of our autonomic nervous system (causing headache, irritable bowel syndrome etc.) and disorders of our hormonal and immune systems (creating susceptibility to infection, chronic fatigue, depression, and autoimmune diseases like rheumatoid arthritis, lupus, and allergies).

So, by not dealing with our stress in the right way, we are doing more damage to ourselves than we can imagine, so even though you think you are just complaining about your life you are probably also doing long term damage to your health.

Asking advice

Keeping your new plans and dreams to yourself is one option. But you can share them with the people that are closest to you. Just make sure that those you do share them with are positive people and that they only have your interests at heart.

Don't just be honest with yourself about your future: ask your closest friends if they can help you achieve your goal. Ask them if they think you are being realistic about what you wish to change. You don't need to take their advice, but they can be a great form of support - but only if it is positive support.

I personally don't associate with negative people. Anyone who is negative, I am polite to but I do not associate with them on a daily, weekly or even a yearly basis if possible. Negativity is a luxury you cannot now afford. You are too busy moving forward with your new life, to your new goals so you just have don't time for negativity. Cut it out of your life.

I have been forced to tell clients that their doctors are wrong from time to time. Especially in cases where the doctor told a client; 'you can't lose weight, that is just your shape get used to it'. Another client was told by a 'fitness' expert that exercise does not help you lose weight, it only tones the body, which any child can tell you is wrong information. I have had clients who thought that sugar gives you energy but that it does not make you fat.

The right of people to have an opinion also means that they have the right to be very, very wrong. Education is a great thing and experts are certainly good for certain issues. However, sometimes the school of life and hard knocks can teach you more and give you more of a gut feeling than any college graduate. So, always go with your gut feeling. It will very rarely be wrong.

Chapter 3

There is no money in Broccoli

When it comes to losing weight, having a healthy lifestyle, living longer, looking better, there is only one person who can motivate you and only person who really cares about you and that is you. This is because there is no money for others in your being healthy. Of course your close family and friends have an interest in your well-being, but at the end of the day we are all alone and responsible for ourselves.

On top of this, every marketing company, advertising company and promotions company in the world spends millions each year to keep you under control. That sounds very '1984' in the George Orwell type of way, but what it means is that companies endeavour to make you buy their products, mostly because the products themselves are not really something you need and are at worst bad for you and your health.

Take the tobacco business; for a long time the biggest sponsorship deals and advertising brands were all funded by the tobacco industry, because they know and now everybody knows that smoking will kill you. So with tobacco advertising culled by Governments worldwide, alcohol sponsorship is next, again because the product is not good for people. However, it's directly due to the fact that it is bad for us that advertisers have to try so hard to make it look like it's cool, hip and trendy. That the beautiful people drink a certain brand and that if you want to be one of them, just buy their beer.

Do you think the big drinks companies who sell beers or wines want to promote health? Do you think the big fast food chains want you healthy? Do you think pharmaceutical companies or undertakers want you healthy? Advertising by its very nature is aimed at selling you things, most of which you don't really need.

Think about it for a second - water from the tap, sunshine, swimming in the sea, fruit, vegetables, walking, jogging, chatting to friends are a few of the things you can do each day and which are good for you and free of charge or very cheap to buy.

No one who advertises wants you to be healthy. Why? Because there is no money in your being healthy. The fatter you are, the more junk food you eat, the more medication you buy, all of these companies are making money from you, once you are unhealthy. An advertiser's dream is for you to be sitting in front of a TV, texting in your vote for a reality TV show through the phone network that is in partnership with the TV company, ordering a pizza by the sponsor of the TV show, drinking a beer made by the sponsor of the sports show that is on directly after the reality TV show.

Have you ever seen big advertising campaigns for Broccoli? There is no money in Broccoli.

Despite the fact it is one of the best things you can eat, known medically as a super food. There is also no money in walking. Despite it is one of the best forms of exercise you can take. Why? Because no one can make money from you going for a walk. Advertising is based on psychology, the psychology of fear and attraction.

At the birth of modern day advertising, who do you think the big companies of Madison Avenue hired to give them the edge over their competitors? Psychologists. One of the most famous was John Watson, the psychologist behind modern day Behaviourism.

Watson denied the existence of any human instincts, capacities, talents or temperaments. He famously said in 1930, 'give me a dozen healthy infants, well-formed and my own specified world to bring them up in and I'll guarantee to take any one of them at random and train him to become any type of specialist I might select, doctor, lawyer, artist, merchant-chief and yes even a beggar man and thief, regardless of his talents, penchants, tendencies, abilities, vocations or the race of his ancestors.' Watson also claimed that people's emotions could be played with by using the psychology behind advertising, including the emotions of love, fear and rage. He was also the first to develop celebrity endorsements for products.

In 1903, Walter Dill Scott published 'The Theory and Practice of Advertising' in which he claimed that people are highly suggestible and obedient. He is credited with giving scientific credibility to psychology's involvement in advertising.

This industry is charged with just one job, to get you to part with your hard earned money to buy products you don't need or sometimes don't really want. Psychology is being used to tap into your subconscious mind on a daily basis. Research from the University of Leicester in the UK showed that in a store where wine was for sale, when they played French music, more French wine was sold. When they played German music, more German wine was sold.

A French study revealed that playing songs with 'pro-social' lyrics about empathy and helping others in restaurants increased tips. Other studies have shown that playing slow music in restaurants encourages diners to linger longer and relax, prompting them to buy an extra drink or dessert. US stores such as Abercrombie and Fitch and others play loud music as this stimulates the nervous system, leading to weakened self-control and more impulsive purchases.

In legal circles, eyewitness testimony has often been discredited as people can be easily persuaded to say they saw things that they did not see. This has been proven time and time again. Now advertisers are using this ability to their benefit by distorting a person's memory and perception of products. McDonald's 'I'm loving it', the Coke slogan 'Coke is it' and Budweiser's 'King of Beers' are just examples of how psychology plays into advertising. Just like L'Oreal claim that 'you're worth it' and pay celebrities millions of dollars to tell you this because the theory is, 'you should trust me, I'm famous.'

It's all a game to get you to buy their products. It's not real and it's just designed to make a fool out of you. Coke is not it, in fact Coke is far from it. Budweiser will not make you cool and trendy, few people in your local bar look like the guys and girls in the advertising for Budweiser. Those who eat McDonald's daily sadly don't look like the models and actors in their advertising.

So from today and for the rest of your remaining 29,200 days, it's time to stop letting yourself be led around by the nose by advertisers. It may sound harsh but as Khaled Hosseini, the novelist and physician, said 'Better to be hurt by the truth than comforted with a lie.'

The pain and pleasure principles

What if you are you having trouble finding your direction? Finding what to write on your list, finding out what to do with the remainder of your 29,000 days? Then it's time to examine the pain and pleasure principle, which may just help you to find the road that is best suited to you. This principle is something that has been around for a long time and relates to the fact that what suits you may not suit someone else and what suits them may not suit you.

In its simplest terms, if you put property millionaire Donald Trump in Calcutta with the poorest and most helpless people in the world, I am sure he would not find too much pleasure in it. However, if you had put Mother Teresa in Trump Tower in New York and asked her to do a multi-million dollar deal, I am sure she would not have found too much pleasure in it either.

Mother Teresa found pleasure in helping the poor in Calcutta, not in doing deals in New York. Donald Trump finds pleasure from doing deals in New York and is unlikely to enjoy living with the poor in Calcutta. Neither of them is right and neither is wrong. It is just that each one of us gets pleasure from some things and pain from the others.

That's why some of us go on camping holidays and others go to the beach. Why some people work for the minimum wage helping people and others work as high powered bankers. There is no right or wrong choice. There is just the choice that suits you personally, the choice that gives you pleasure and in which you can avoid pain.

So remember what I asked you in Chapter 1, what would you do for free? What job or career would you do without getting paid? Where would you live if you had the choice? What car would you drive? Would you be single or married, which would suit you better?

Virginia Woolf once said; 'You cannot find peace by avoiding life' so get moving today. The days are still ticking down. Jonathan Swift said 'May you live every day of your life'. While George Bernard Shaw said 'A life spent making mistakes is not only more honourable, but more useful than a life spent doing nothing.'

Is the message going into your mind at this stage, are you getting the sense of urgency that life is showing you? The days are ticking down. It's time to change.

Laughter really is the best medicine

Over the years I have carried out a lot of research into the effects of humour on those living with cancer. With groups of cancer patients, I have found that stress and anxiety has been significantly reduced by the power of humour. In order for your life to change, you must accept that a smile really can change your day and the day of those around you.

Humour therapy was first explained and developed by Norman Cousins in his book *Anatomy of an Illness*. Cousins claimed that for every ten minutes of laughter he gained two hours of pain free sleep. Dr. William Fry, associate professor of clinical psychiatry at Stanford University, has studied the effects of laughter for 30 years and compares laughter to 'inner jogging,' and claims that laughing 100 times a day is the equivalent of 10 minutes of rowing a boat. According to Fry, laughter increases the heart rate, improves blood circulation, and works muscles all over the body.

Research in recent years suggests that laughter has a physiological effect on the body. It releases endorphins, which are the body's natural painkillers and this in turn leads to protection from depression. Studies from the Department of Clinical Immunology at Loma Linda University School of Medicine in California have shown that laughter 'decreases serum cortisol levels, increases T lymphocytes, and increases the number of natural killer cells'. This implies that laughter stimulates the immune system.

It has also been demonstrated that humour and laughter have a psychological impact. Herbert Lefcourt, a psychologist at the University of Waterloo, studied the effects of humour on dealing with change and our emotional response to stress. Results of his work have shown that the ability to sense and appreciate humour can buffer the mood disturbances that happen in response to negative life events.

Participants who viewed a 90 minute humorous video showed a decrease in cortisol (which suppresses the immune system) and growth hormone with laughter. In addition, levels of adrenaline (epinephrine) were lower in the experimental laughter group. In one study, complementary therapies – such as prayer, humour and support groups - were used on cancer patients with 87% showing a positive response.

Psychologist Aaron Beck showed humorous material to individuals and found an increase in natural killer cell activity (NKCA) and Immunoglobulins G, A and M. It has also been shown that people who used humour as a coping strategy reported having fewer health problems than those who did not.

Laughter in relation to pain thresholds has also been tested and after watching a 20 minute funny video, laughter significantly increased participants' pain thresholds and therefore was considered to be as effective as relaxation.

The importance of laughter during group meetings was shown to have a positive effect, according to women with breast cancer. Participants who viewed humorous material showed a higher pain threshold then those who watched non-humorous material. Women who had been given a breast cancer diagnosis and survived reported that humour increased their coping skills and spirituality. In relation to cancer in general, studies have shown that the more people laugh, the higher the increase in NKCA. This in turn helps in the fight to stop the formation of clusters of cancer cells.

A study in 2010 examined the effectiveness of a humour therapy program in relieving chronic pain, enhancing happiness and life satisfaction, and reducing loneliness among older people with chronic pain. Older residents of a nursing home were invited to join an 8-week humour therapy programme (experimental group), while those in another nursing home were treated as a control group and were not offered the programme.

There were 36 older people in the experimental group and 34 in the control group. Upon completion of the humour therapy program, there were significant decreases in pain and perception of loneliness for the experimental group, and significant increases in happiness and life satisfaction. These changes were not seen in the control group.

The use of humour therapy appears to be an effective non-pharmacological intervention strategy. A study in Japan showed that NKCA increased with laughter in the experimental group who watched humorous material but NKCA levels stayed the same in the control group.

The Clinical Journal of Oncology Nursing revealed in another report that not only was humour a coping mechanism but it improved pain thresholds and elevated natural killer cells while having a positive effect on the immune system.

The strongest evidence for the relationship between cancer and stress can be found in the work of Dr Anil Sood from the University of Texas, as published in *The Journal of Clinical Investigation*. He endorsed previous claims that stress promotes cancer indirectly by weakening the immune system's anti-tumour defence system or by encouraging new tumour-feeding blood vessels to form. This shows that stress hormones, such as adrenaline (epinephrine) can directly support tumour growth and spread.

His study of eighty cases of human ovarian cancer grouped together showed that patient stress along with elevated stress hormone activity were associated with higher levels of activated Focal Adhesion Kinase (FAK), a protein which is linked to faster disease progression.

According to Dr Sood, 'for normal cells to thrive in the body they need to be attached to their neighbours and their surroundings'. Cells that detach from their environment undergo a form of programmed cell death called anoikis. But cancer cells have come up with a way to bypass this effect, and they avoid anoikis.

This allows cancer cells to break off from tumours, spread throughout the body (in blood or other fluid) and form new tumours at distant sites (metastasis). Sood then studied the effect of stress hormones on human ovarian cancer cell anoikis. 'Cells that were exposed to stress hormones were protected from self destruction meaning they could survive without being anchored to their surroundings but this was only in vitro.' Sood and his team then extended their findings into a mouse model of cancer. They transplanted ovarian cancer cells into a mouse and restrained the mouse to cause stress levels to increase. Their tumours grew more quickly than in a control group of mice.

So your behaviour on a day to day basis can affect your long term quality and length of your life. You may even be able to increase the number of days you live by laughing daily.

Reliability

So far in this chapter we have focused on the changes you will make to the psychology of who you are. You have read about how you are the only person who has your interest at heart. You have learnt about the pain and pleasure principles, you understand that what is suitable for you may not be good for someone else, and that's just fine. Finally, we have learnt that enjoying each day by laughing will not only make you smile but may also increase the length and quality of your life.

So to end this chapter, I want to talk to you about reliability and follow through. So far, I have explained to you how the mind works, how you are in charge of your destiny and how you are responsible for your own life. Now we are moving onto the inspiration you are going to need in order for you to move to the next step in your action plan. Reliability is the next thing you need to instil in your own personality. No one will deal or put up with someone who is unreliable. There is little point in you writing down the list of things you are going to do and then not doing any of them. So we must have follow through. Remember, if you do the things you have always done, you will get the same results over again.

From now on, you must be reliable when it comes to your word. If you say you will lose weight, get a new job, find love, travel the world, write a book, learn the piano etc., from now on you must write it down and commit to it without hesitation.

For ten years I worked as a professional journalist for the biggest newspaper in Ireland, I was never the best writer in the world, I never had the best connections or a degree from the best journalism school. But, by the age of 26 I was writing the most widely read column of any newspaper in Ireland with over one million readers every week, mostly due to the fact that I was reliable. When I left journalism to train as a psychologist, I set up a wedding band with some friends to pay my way through years of University. The band performed at over 1,000 weddings because we were reliable.

Anyone I worked with in either the media or music industry who was unreliable, was cut. Full stop. If someone let me down on a story, that was it, they were cut out of the loop. If a singer or musician let the band down, they were cut. It may see harsh, but remember it's not show friends, it's show business. Those within the entertainment industry have one mantra 'The show must go on' and it does.

Your reliability, your word and your follow through on what you say you will do must be as strong as Oak, if you are to be a success in life. Winners only deal with other winners. If you say you are going to do something, then do it. Don't just talk about doing it.

Entrepreneur Nolan Bushnell says 'The critical ingredient is getting off your butt and doing something. It's as simple as that. A lot of people have ideas, but there are few who decide to do something about them now. Not tomorrow. Not next week. But today. The true entrepreneur is a doer, not a dreamer.'

Every successful business person you talk to will tell you the same thing. You need to go and get the opportunities, they don't come to you. The important thing is not to be afraid to take a chance. Then once you find that something you love, aim to be the best at it. There will be no limits to what you can achieve, only the limits you set for yourself, so aim high.

The greatest TV chat show host of all time, Oprah Winfrey, who overcame all the odds to become a billionaire said 'I feel that luck is preparation meeting opportunity.' So being reliable and focused today means that you are ready to saddle your dreams tomorrow.

Reminder

It's time again to reinforce that new image you want for yourself. Remember from now on to see that image of yourself as you want to be, when you press your left finger and thumb together. Do it now and see the newly successful you in the mirror getting closer. Now, you are ready to start the journey, to the next step. It is not a case of 'if' you are going to become the successful person you want and deserve to be, but 'when' you become that person.

Many have come before you and in the next chapter I am going to tell you about the success stories of many people who grew up in harder times, with less money and less education then we have today. People that overcame bigger odds, bigger hurdles, bigger problems and worse economic times then we are living through today.

Don't be disillusioned if you have yet to finalise what you want in life, there is still have plenty of time for you to focus on your list of goals. Just keep in mind the fact that when you wake up every morning, the days are still ticking away. All the stories I have shared with you and all the words of wisdom from those who have come before you echo with the same advice. Do it now, today, this minute. Tomorrow waits for no one.

Chapter 4

Pilgrims get shot

The media business is one of the toughest in the world. One publisher I worked for lived by the mantra that 'pilgrims get shot, while settlers survive.'

So, you can take it from now on that no matter what you want to do, someone else has done it before you, which has left a blueprint for you to follow. That's not saying that every now and then an original idea cannot make millions, it can. By using the guidelines that those before you have laid down you can learn from their successes but also from their failures.

Your journey is now beginning. There will be stumbling blocks, detours and some heartache. I have included below a list of some of the most successful people in history. Each one of the following men failed and failed again before finally making a name for themselves in the world.

> Henry Ford ended up broke five times before making a success of his Ford motor company, the only way he finally succeeded was by hiring men for twice the money his competitors paid.
>
> R. H. Macy, the man behind Macy's department store in New York, failed with 7 businesses before finding great success with his New York store.
>
> Soichiro Honda started his billion dollar business after Toyota turned him down for a job as an engineer. He went

out alone and started building scooters from his home.

Akio Morita started his company, Sony, whose first product was a rice cooker which failed to cook rice and only sold 100 units.

Microsoft boss Bill Gates had a computer start-up company called Traf-O-Data, with his friend Paul Allen, which failed. The duo then had another go and started Microsoft.

Harland David Sanders, better known as Colonel Sanders of Kentucky Fried Chicken fame, received over 1,000 rejections of his secret recipe for chicken before a restaurant finally accepted it.

Walt Disney's first few companies went bankrupt before he made his millions by developing the character Mickey Mouse for his first cartoon, Steamboat Willie.

Albert Einstein did not speak until his was four and could not read until he was seven. He was also refused entry into the Zurich Polytechnic School.

Charles Darwin was called lazy by his father, while Isaac Newton failed so badly at running his family farm that his uncle took over and sent him to college to get an education.

Thomas Edison was told he was too stupid to learn anything in school. On top of that he was fired from his first two jobs, he then made over 1,000 inventions most of which did not work, before he found one that worked. That one just happened to be the light bulb.

Two of the most famous brothers in history - Orville and Wilbur Wright - battled depression and illness. Having opened a small bicycle shop, they then tried to make their inventions fly. They failed many times, before finally getting one to stay in the air. This of course became the birth of the aeroplane.

Even great leaders have had their failures. Winston Churchill struggled in school and failed his final year. He was sacked from one government job and lost just about every election. He never gave up and finally made it to be Prime Minister at the age of 62. He also won the Nobel Prize for Literature.

Abraham Lincoln was one of the greatest American Presidents. However, he went off to war as a Captain and came home a Private. He then started and failed at a number of businesses, before finally being successful in politics after countless defeats.

Oprah Winfrey was fired from her job as a TV reporter because her boss said that she was 'unfit for TV'.

Former US Vice President Dick Cheney flunked out of Yale University not once but twice, which led to George Bush telling him; 'if you graduate from Yale you become President, but if you flunk out you will only make it to be Vice-President'.

Some big Hollywood names have fallen at the first hurdle. Jerry Seinfeld, the famous comic, walked out on stage for his first gig in the comedy club, froze and was laughed off. But, he came back the next night and the rest is history.

Fred Astaire was told during his first screen test; 'you can't act and you can't sing, you are slightly bald and can dance a little'.

Oscar winner Sidney Poitier was told at his first audition to go home and stop wasting people's time and that he should go out and become a dishwasher or something.

Hollywood studio chiefs turned down Charlie Chaplin when he first arrived, saying that his act was to nonsensical to ever sell.

Lucille Ball was told by her own drama teacher to try another profession.

Harrison Ford was told in his first movie role that simply didn't have what it takes to make it.

Marilyn Monroe was told by model agents to become a secretary and not a model.

Vincent Van Gogh only ever sold one painting while he was alive and that was to a friend.

One of the best stories about success comes from Stephen Spielberg, who was rejected by his choice of film school. He then went on the Universal studious backstage tour, got off half way around, walked out the main gate in a suit, saying goodbye to the security guard, then returning the next day and the next day, getting to know people on the set. Eventually he got a job for real in the studio. By that stage he had even found himself an office.

Stephen King had thrown his script for Carrie in the trash after 30 rejections, when his wife took it out and today he is one of the best-selling authors of all time.

Harry Potter author J. K. Rowling was a single mother on welfare, depressed and penniless before her persistence finally paid off.

Author Jack London was in an even worse state and got over 600 rejection letters before finally being published.

Mozart died near broke after being fired from a position as a court musician in Salzburg.

Elvis Presley was told in 1954 by a promoter to go back to driving his truck because he was not going to make it as a singer.

The Beatles were told by their first record company that they didn't like their music and that guitar music was on the way out.

The world's most famous and successful basketball player, Michael Jordan, was cut from his high school basketball team.

If they can make it so can you

In 2008, authors Brett and Kate McKay wrote an amazing article about 25 of the Greatest Self-Made Men in American History, I have included parts of it here as it really is a testimony that anyone can overcome the odds, no matter where they come from, to make it to the top of the mountain of life.

One of the men on their list is Benjamin Franklin, one of the founding fathers of modern America, who was the 15th of 17 children born to a candle-maker. His accomplishments are too many to mention but by the end of his life he had been a successful author and inventor before becoming a councilman, postmaster and speaker of the Pennsylvania State House. Not bad for the son of a candle-maker.

Another self made man is Ross Perot, who was born to a father who worked as a cotton broker. After leaving the Navy, Perot became a salesman for IBM. Perot quickly distinguished himself from the pack, filling the year's sales quota in two weeks. Full of entrepreneurial ideas, but ignored by his superiors, Perot left IBM in 1962 to found his own company, Electronic Data Systems.

Things started off rocky; Perot's initial attempts to sell their data processing services to corporations resulted in 77 rejections. Yet, Perot persisted, and won government contracts for EDS, turning the company into an Information Technology powerhouse. EDS was eventually bought by GM for a cool $700 million.

Not content to rest on his business laurels, Perot began to involve himself in political policy issues, an interest that culminated in his famous run for the presidency in 1992. Garnering the largest percentage of the popular vote as a third party candidate since Theodore Roosevelt ran in 1912, Perot's success surprised the pundits.

John D. Rockefeller needed neither a trust fund nor the example of a successful father to become the richest man in American history. His dad was a salesman who was rarely at home as young John grew up. Rockefeller was left to forge his own path. As a young man, he took a job as an assistant bookkeeper, saved his dough, and then partnered with others in buying a couple of oil refineries in Cleveland. In 1870, Rockefeller incorporated his holdings into Standard Oil.

Rockefeller's business plan was simple; by obsessively increasing the efficiency of his refineries and pressuring rail-road companies for discounted shipping, he successfully undercut and then bought out the competition. It was said that he had the 'soul of a bookkeeper,' and he loved to pore over his figures and see where waste could be eliminated. Rockefeller soon owned nearly every division of the oil business and controlled 90% of the kerosene market. Such success netted Rockefeller great wealth; when he retired he was estimated to have accumulated a $1,500,000,000 fortune. Having won this wealth through his own toil, he didn't just sit on this money. He donated much of it in the hope of providing others with similar opportunities for success.

Designer Ralph Lauren grew up as a Jewish kid in the Bronx, Lauren never hung out at the country club, played polo, or went sailing on a yacht. Although his brand is now a famous symbol of gentility and affluence, Lauren's own beginnings were far more humble. Born as Ralph Rueben Lifshitz, his parents were Ashkenazi Jews who had immigrated from Belarus, and his father was a house painter. The family lived in a small apartment, with Ralph sharing a room with his two brothers. Ralph's mother hoped he would become a rabbi, but from an early age, Lauren was drawn to fashion and entrepreneurship.

While at school, he worked after class as a stock boy and sold handmade ties to his classmates in order to purchase stylish suits. Lauren attended Baruch College for two years, but then dropped out. He never went to fashion school. After a stint in the army, he became a salesman for Brooks Brothers. They weren't interested in helping Lauren develop his own line of ties, so he then went to work for Beau Brumwell Neckwear where he was allowed to design and sell his own 'Polo' brand of ties in their showroom.

The ties became popular and other stores started carrying them. Lauren started designing women's and men's wear, and introduced his now famous Polo shirt. He soon had enough money to open his own store and develop his brand into an empire. Today, Lauren has 35 boutiques across the US, has expanded his brand to include home furnishings and cologne, and currently ranks as the 76th richest man in America.

Frederick Douglass is the ultimate rags to riches stories since there are no rags lowlier than those worn by American slaves. Rising from the shackles of slavery to extraordinary success required monumental amounts of hard work, tenacity and passion, and Frederick Douglass had these qualities in spades. Douglass understood that nothing in life would ever be handed to him. When his master's wife, who had been teaching him the alphabet, was reprimanded for doing so by her husband, Douglass continued to learn to read by interacting with white children and working through any written materials he could find.

When he was traded to the cruel mastery of Edward Covey, who regularly whipped Douglass, Douglass confronted his master, getting him to back down and never raise his hand to him again.

In 1838, Douglass took his greatest risk yet and escaped from slavery to Massachusetts. Douglass soon rose to prominence, becoming an outspoken abolitionist, a spectacular orator, a best-selling author, and a newspaper publisher. After the Civil War, Douglass served as President of the Freedman's Savings Bank, Marshal of the District of Columbia, minister-resident and consul-general to the Republic of Haiti, and Chargé D'affaires for the Dominican Republic. During the 1888 Republican Convention, he became the first African-American to receive a vote to be nominated for the Presidency. Dying in 1895, Douglass had risen from slavery to become one of the most prominent and well-respected men in the United States.

Mr McDonalds, Ray Kroc, a high school dropout, attained his first job by employing a bit of dishonesty; the 15 year old young man lied to the military to become an ambulance driver during World War I. The war ended before young Ray could see action, and so Kroc took a job playing piano for a radio station at night and selling paper cups by day. He next became fascinated with a multi-mixer milkshake machine and purchased the marketing rights to it. For the next 17 years, Kroc travelled the country selling his milkshake making miracle to whoever would listen. As he made the rounds to customers, he became intrigued by a small chain of hamburger restaurants in San Bernardino, California owned by the McDonald brothers, who bought more of his milkshake machines than anyone else.

While the McDonald brothers were satisfied with their small franchise, Kroc believed the burger business had far greater potential. Although Kroc was by then a 53 year old man suffering from diabetes and arthritis and missing both his thyroid gland and gall bladder, he had a vision of turning the restaurant into a global fast food empire. In 1961, he purchased the McDonald's franchise. In only a few years, Kroc had sold a billion hamburgers and opened the franchise's 500th store. McDonald's had begun its campaign to take over the world.

Thomas Edison was kicked out of school for being easily distracted and he received only 3 months of formal schooling. The rest of Edison's education came from his mother's home-schooling and his reading of classic books. Though he lost nearly all of his hearing at a young age, Edison did not let the disability hinder him. Early on he showed a tenacious entrepreneurial streak; he sold candy and newspapers aboard trains as a youth and then won a position as telegraph operator when he saved a station agent's son from being run over by a train. As a telegrapher, he worked 12 hours a day, 6 days a week.

Edison requested the night shift so that he could read and do his experiments during the slow evening hours. His constant tinkering paid off; Edison (often with help from his partners) came up with a myriad of inventions, including the phonograph and most famously, the first commercially viable incandescent lamp. 'The Wizard of Menlo Park' was both a genius inventor and a savvy business man; he filed more than 1,500 patents during his lifetime and founded 14 companies, including General Electric.

Larry Ellison was born in the Bronx to an unwed mother; he never knew his father. While still an infant, Ellison was shipped off to Chicago to be taken care of and eventually adopted by his mother's aunt and uncle. Ellison grew up in a two bedroom apartment and attended two years of college before dropping out when his adoptive mother died. Interested in computers and software design, Ellison went to work for Ampex Corporation before founding what would become the database company Oracle in 1977 with $2,000 of his own money. Greatly successful, the company made Ellison a billionaire many times over and continues to secure his place as the 5th richest man in the world.

Abraham Lincoln became one of the greatest American presidents, but his life was not all plain sailing. He lacked connections, charisma, good looks and formal education. Born in a one-room cabin to uneducated farmer parents, Abraham Lincoln's rise to the Presidency has long been the stuff of legend.

Lincoln was almost entirely self-educated; he received only 18 months of formal schooling. He offset this disadvantage by voraciously consuming any book he could get his hands on. At age 22, Lincoln packed his belongings into a canoe and paddled out on his own. He taught himself the law and became a successful attorney and state legislator in Illinois. Losing his senatorial campaign in 1858 to Stephen Douglas did not deter him from his goals; he persevered against this very same opponent to win the presidency. The rest, of course, is history. Lincoln went on to guide America through her darkest and stormiest hour.

The idea for Wal-Mart came from the mind of an unassuming farm boy from Oklahoma called Sam Walton. Walton spent his early years living on his family's farm, and then moved to Missouri when his father decided to become a farm loan appraiser. Sam showed great ambition from an early age; he became Missouri's youngest ever Eagle Scout when he received that award in 8th grade, and he was elected class president during his senior year in high school.

Despite growing up during the Great Depression and working odd jobs such as delivering newspapers to help support his family, Walton excelled academically throughout his school years. He paid his way through the University of Missouri by working as a lifeguard, newspaper delivery boy, and waiter. When he graduated, he took jobs at JCPenney and at a DuPont munitions plant before serving in the army during World War II.

After the war, Walton was determined to open his own variety store. He pooled the substantial amount of money he saved while in the military and, with a loan from his father-in-law, bought a Ben Franklin store in Newport, Arkansas. Walton supplied customers with a wide variety of goods at low prices and kept those prices low by buying in high volume directly from wholesalers. The store was highly successful, and Walton then opened his own store -Walton's Five & Dime - in Bentonville. In 1962, Walton introduced the first true Wal-Mart to Rogers, Arkansas. That store, like all his others, turned a nice profit, and Walton began to expand the franchise across the country, making it the world's largest retailer by 1991. He reigned as America's richest man from 1985-1988, and were he still alive today, he would be the world's richest man, with a wealth double that of Bill Gates.

Some men get into the Oval office the easy way and some don't. Harry S. Truman was an example of the latter and lived by the motto: 'The buck stops here', long before it officially adorned his

Oval Office desk. Such decisiveness was a necessary trait for a man who had to routinely overcome low expectations to win respect.

Truman was born into a farming family in Missouri. After leaving high school, he was employed in a few odd jobs before returning to labour on the family farm. College was not in the cards for Harry; he couldn't afford to attend any school except West Point, and they turned him down because of his poor eyesight. Truman would thus become the only president to serve after 1897 who did not hold a college degree.

Yet, Harry was determined to make the best of his circumstances. He joined the National Guard and served in World War I. His eyesight should have prevented him from joining up, but Truman memorised the chart in order to pass the test. Truman served heroically, and became a Colonel in the Guard. After the war, Truman opened a haberdashery in Kansas City that went bankrupt during a recession in 1921. He was then elected as a county judge. In 1934, he became a US Senator. Ten years later, he was chosen to be Franklin Roosevelt's Vice-President. When FDR died, Truman had finally ascended to the highest office in the land.

When he ran for re-election in 1948, Truman was, as he had been in his senatorial campaigns, the true underdog. He had to fight fiercely just to secure the nomination, and during the general election, he was determined to get his message out to the people and he crisscrossed the nation in an energetic whistle-stop tour. While the Democrat's prospects looked bleak, Truman vigorously came from behind and pulled off an upset win. He had spent his whole life giving his naysayers hell, and he had done so once again.

Modern music would not be the same without Sean 'Puff Daddy' Combs who most deserves the title of self-made man. Mr. Combs claims to work harder than anyone else in the entertainment business, and he has the success to show for it. Born in public housing projects in Harlem, Sean's father was shot to death when Sean was only 2. At age 12, Combs, who was too young to officially have his own paper round, found a way around the rule by taking over the routes of several older boys and giving them 50% of his earnings. He was soon making over $700 a week as a paperboy. After high school, Combs interned at Uptown Records while he attended Howard University. He dropped out and took an executive position with the company. Fired from the label in 1993, Combs formed his own company - Bad Boy Records.

In addition to producing hit artists like the Notorious B.I.G., Combs started putting out his own successful rap records and diversifying his business interests. His enterprises now include the Sean John clothing line, a cologne, the Making the Band television series, and a restaurant in Atlanta. He is now worth an estimated $324 million.

Very few men will ever have the chance to completely revolutionise the American way of life; even fewer who do so come from obscure backgrounds. Henry Ford's name keeps popping up when anyone tries to write about those who made it against all the odds. He was born in 1863 on a farm near Detroit, Michigan. His father wanted Henry to take over the family farm, but Henry had other plans. At

16, he left home to become a machinist's apprentice. After several years, he returned to farm work, and he also ran a sawmill. But his love for engineering kept calling him away.

In 1891, Ford was hired by the Edison Illuminating Company, and he worked his way up to be Chief Engineer. He saved money scrupulously until he had enough so he could quit and work on his experiments with gasoline engines. Ford began creating and testing self-propelled vehicles, but he could not produce them as cheaply and efficiently as he desired. With this goal in mind, Ford and partner Alexander Malcomson founded Ford Motor Company. Ford's technical smarts were matched by his business savvy.

Ford had to offer his auto workers $5 for a day's work, nearly double the going rate, to get the right staff. The country's best mechanics flocked to Ford, and this greatly increased productivity and slowed employee turnover. He introduced moving assembly belts to his plants, which greatly improved efficiency. Such ideas helped make the Model T an affordable, immediate, and widespread success; half of all cars on the road in 1918 came from Ford factories. Ford found equal success with his next model, the Model A, which he had played large part in designing. Ford secured sole ownership of the company for his family, expanded the business internationally, reaped a massive fortune, and introduced America to its ongoing love affair with the automobile.

Acting and politics was never going to be an easy combination, but any man who can turn an acting career into a successful run for the presidency certainly earns the title of self-made man. There was no silver spoon in the mouth of Ronald Reagan when he came into the world in 1911. Born in Tampico, Illinois, Reagan's father was a salesman who was always looking for better work.

Reagan thus grew up moving from one tiny town in Illinois to the next, often living in apartments above banks and stores. After college, he became a radio announcer and landed a film contract with Warner Brothers. After a stint in the military, Reagan became the president of the Screen Actors Guild. He began his foray into politics by working on Barry Goldwater's Presidential campaign in 1964. Then in 1966, without having held prior political office, Reagan was elected governor of California. Although he failed to win the Republican nomination for the presidency in 1976, Reagan was not discouraged and won not only the nomination, but also the White House in 1980.

Another name that pops up again and again in every success book is that of Andrew Carnegie, who represents the epitome of the self-made man. His father was a Scottish hand-loom weaver, who moved with his family to America in 1848 when Andrew was 13. Carnegie's first job was working as a bobbin boy at a textile factory, earning $1.50 a week. He subsequently took jobs as a boiler tender, bookkeeper's clerk, and telegraph delivery boy. All the while he read to educate himself and worked to mitigate his thick Scottish accent. In 1853, Carnegie landed a job with the Pennsylvania Telegraph Company.

He religiously saved his money and reinvested it in the rail-road business. He worked his way up to being superintendent of the

Pennsylvania Railroad's Western Division and then supervised the Union's telegraph lines during the Civil War. He continued to make very wise investments with his savings, which reaped him handsome dividends. After the war, he left the rail-road business and began to focus on building and investing in ironworks. By bringing great efficiency to the business, taking over one steel company after another, and utilizing vertical integration, Carnegie soon created an empire of steel and iron.

In 1901, Carnegie sold his steel holdings to J. P. Morgan for $480 million. Carnegie had long preached what he called 'The Gospel of Wealth,' a philosophy in which a man should aim to acquire as much fortune as possible and then give it away to others. On this point, (unlike several others), Carnegie was a man of his word. During his lifetime he donated $350,695,653 to philanthropic causes; on his death he gave away the last $30,000,000 of his wealth.

Who said there is no money in chocolate? Milton S. Hershey had to face some bitter failure before he was able to achieve sweet success. Hershey was born on a farm in Pennsylvania in 1857. Due to his father's frequent failed business schemes, the family moved regularly, and Milton's parents separated. Hershey dropped out of school after the fourth grade. He was then apprenticed to a printer, but did not take to that line of work. He began an apprenticeship with a candy maker and after four years learning the trade, he attempted to open his own shop. This venture failed as did his two subsequent efforts in New York City and Chicago. At 28, he returned home to Pennsylvania as an unemployed man who had thus far failed to make anything of his life. But Hershey's luck would soon change; he started a caramel company and this time, his delicious confections caught on.

During his visit to the 1893 World's Columbian Exposition in Chicago, Hershey became fascinated by the German chocolate making machines. He purchased them for his Lancaster caramel factory and began producing various chocolate confections. Sensing the great potential in chocolate treats, Hershey sold his successful caramel company in 1900 for $1,000,000. With this new wealth, he bought 40,000 acres of land near Lancaster, Pennsylvania and built the world's largest chocolate factory and a model town for his employees. He was determined to bring what was then a Swiss luxury product - milk chocolate - to the masses.

Walt Disney, the man who would one day create the 'happiest place on earth,' experienced a less than idyllic childhood. His father wandered from one job to another looking to find success, and often relied on his brother to stay afloat. Walt lacked not just financial security, but also affection; his father was a cold and abusive man. Walt was determined to blaze his own path of success and not end up like his dad.

At 16, he dropped out of high school and served in the ambulance corps during World War I. After the war, Disney found work creating advertisements for businesses in Kansas City. He was fascinated by the emerging field of animation and decided to set up his own animation business. He was not yet able to manage money effectively, and the business went bankrupt. Disney then set up a studio in Hollywood and began turning out cartoons, culminating in the enormously popular *Steamboat Willie* in 1928. Over the next several years, Disney introduced equally beloved characters such as Donald Duck, Goofy and Pluto. In 1934, Disney began to work on his most ambitious idea yet - a full-length animated feature. Dubbed 'Disney's folly' by his critics, most thought the idea would spell the demise of the Disney studio.

Instead, Snow White and the Seven Dwarfs was a smashing success. The film was followed by a myriad of other beloved full-length features and animated shorts. In the 1950s, Disney expanded the work of his company to include the production of live-action films. Disney also completed an ambitious project few believed could be a success - the 1955 opening of Disneyland in California. Disneyworld followed in 1964. Walt always understood the desires of average people. While critics lamented the artificially wholesome world depicted in his family-friendly movies and theme parks, the public fell in love with it and bought completely into Disney's vision.

Today, there are still stories like those mentioned above. One man who has changed the modern world is Barack Obama. His childhood was far from typical. Obama was born to a white mother and Kenyan father in Hawaii. His father went back to Kenya when he was only 2 and saw his son only once more. His mother married again, this time to an Indonesian, and the family moved to Indonesia. Barack lived there for several years and then returned to Hawaii to live with his grandparents.

Obama graduated from Columbia University, worked as a community organiser in Chicago for 3 years and then went to Harvard Law School. While there he became the first African-American to be elected president of the Harvard Law Review. Obama returned to Chicago and spent 12 years as a professor at the University of Chicago Law School. He was elected to the Illinois State Senate in 1996 and the US Senate in 2004. After less than one term as Senator, Obama won the presidential election and became the first black president in United States history.

To prove that there is money in any field you just have to look at two one-off millionaires, Ben Cohen and Jerry Greenfield were childhood buddies who early on bonded over their preference for eating over attending gym class. After High School, Ben attended and dropped out of several colleges, never quite finding his calling. He eventually took a job teaching pottery on a farm in the Adirondack Mountains. Jerry attended and graduated from Oberlin College. Upon graduation, he unsuccessfully applied for admission to medical school. When the guys met up again, both were rather adrift professionally. They decided to open an ice cream shop in Burlington, Vermont.

After taking a $5 correspondence course on ice cream making, they opened their store in a dilapidated gas station. The guys' rich, chunky ice cream gained a popular following in the community. They soon began selling pints of their ice cream to local grocery stores. During the next several years, Ben and Jerry were able to expand their franchise and by 1988 they had stores in 18 states. Ben and Jerry's became a nationally known brand, and the company was bought by Unilever in 2000 for $326 million.

Finally, we learn about a modern day rags to riches story. Arnold Schwarzenegger made the improbable leap from bodybuilder and actor to politician. Arnold was born in a small village in Austria. His cold and abusive father was the local police chief, but money was always tight for the family. Life in the unhappy household left Arnold determined to leave home and find fame and fortune. He decided at an early age to make bodybuilding a career.

Schwarzenegger started pumping iron at age 14. He also studied psychology to better sharpen his mind's strength and willpower. Nothing could keep Schwarzenegger from his love of bodybuilding: as a youth he busted into the gym when it was closed on weekends and as a soldier he went AWOL to enter a competition.

Years of sweat and toil paid off when Arnold, at 20, became the youngest ever winner of the Mr. Universe competition, a title he would win four more times. He continued training while simultaneously attending business school and working at a gym. At 21, he moved to America to become a star of the silver screen. He continued to compete in bodybuilding and won the Mr. Olympia title seven times.

Arnold's entrance into film was far more difficult than his workouts. With a thick accent and bulking body, he met many rejections before finally landing roles. After becoming a blockbuster action-star, Schwarzenegger's next obstacle to conquer was politics. In 2003, overcoming his inexperience, accent, and having appeared as Mr. Freeze in *Batman and Robin*, Arnold won the California recall election and became the Governor of California.

Thanks to Brett and Kate McKay for great research on the above stories on how anyone, no matter where you come from, can make a lasting name for themselves in the world.

Chapter 5

All things are possible

The interesting thing about the previous chapter is that everyone mentioned had the same 29,000 days as you do. Look what they did with theirs.

It is never too late or too early to start to follow your dreams. Never mind what others say. These other people, let's call them 'Dream Stealers' are mostly jealous of people who are doing something they cannot or will not do themselves.

Some would call these people 'toxic.' The sad thing is that sometimes these people can even be your own friends or parents. Parents think they know what's best for their own children in order to stop them being hurt. It just happens that some parents don't have the skills, actions or knowledge to help you assess your options and see your vision.

Once you saddle your dreams and never give up on them, you will notice that you will start to have more fun in your life. Who would not like more fun in their life?

Jack Canfield, one of the great motivational speakers said once 'you can't hire someone else to do your push ups for you'. This is one of the best lines I have ever heard. You need to focus your own time on your goal. You need to plan your own day in order to find the time to reach your goal, taking a step towards it every day. Some people just let life go by, living in a 'numb' state. The only thing you should avoid is bad news and toxic people; you should embrace everything else in life that is positive.

Optimism is a frame of mind. It is a glorious skill to have, once you have it. Without it, everything is worthless and nothing is worthwhile. Negative and toxic people have no optimism. They spend their lives complaining about everything, while doing nothing to change their own situation.

The only difference between those who are positive and optimistic, and those who are negative and pessimistic, is their frame of mind and how they look at situations. Leaders always promise that the future will be brighter and we always listen to them.

Churchill once stood up and said: 'I am an optimist, it does not seem too much use being anything else'.

There is also a golden rule, some books have called it *The Secret*, others the *Power of Positive Thinking*, but it goes under many guises. The rule is simple. We reap what we sow. Thc morc you work at something the better the results we get for it.

Just like an exam, the more we study, the better we do. The more you exercise, the healthier you get. Once you take responsibility for yourself, once you understand this one rule, all of a sudden things will start to change for you. From that minute, your life will be different. It encapsulates karma and hard work. It makes you a human magnet, you simply attract everything that you deserve once you work hard for it.

Some call it self-improvement. It involves going out of your way to compliment and praise those around you. It involves being liked and respected by others and having a sense of humour. It involves being thoughtful and courteous to those around you and treating everyone as equals. It involves educating yourself by reading good books, watching good plays, enjoying good art, all of which can be found at little or no cost by using libraries, museums and other low cost or free services. This self-improvement comes from qualities essential for success including dependability and promptness.

Once you are a well-organised person, you are ready for anything that life throws at you. You are ready and willing to accept every opportunity. You are ready to say 'yes' at short notice. You are ready to jump, while others are still finding their feet.

In military circles, they always have what's known as a 'grab bag.' This is a bag that is constantly ready for them to pick up and walk out the door within seconds' warning. Once we have the temperament to be successful and the reliability and drive to be successful, we then need the goal to be successful at.

We will explore this in more detail in following chapters but in essence it involves having that definite goal in life, while also planning to attain that goal in a certain time scale. This is the first step. You will meet issues which get in the way of your goal, but that's fine, you will just go around them or even go through them. Because from now on each day is a new day, a new challenge, and you will approach each day for what it is - a blessing. Another day to do not just what you have to do but what you want to do. No complaining, no bitching, no negativity, just a daily dose of happiness and success. For remember that tomorrow may never come.

One important issue before we move onto setting that goal is that if your goal is money, this may not bring you happiness. Remember, if I locked you in a room full of cash and gold, you could not do anything with it. You could not talk to it, you could not eat it, you could not survive by just having money.

Money alone cannot bring happiness, reduce stress and anxiety or get rid of fear. Money may be nothing but trouble for you. In psychology, lots of research has been done about those who have more money than they could ever spend. From business tycoons to lottery winners, there has been one universal fact that comes up about people and money. It really only has one use and this use will shock you. All the millionaire, billionaires, self made people, world leaders and Wall Street traders who have become rich will only ever get one use for money, in which it will benefit them. That is in giving it away.

Philanthropic ideology is the number one benefit for having money, time and time again. Those who make lots of money eventually give it away to those less fortunate than themselves. Because psychologically that's the only thing it is actually good for. Research has shown that those who give away money become happier people, who live full lives. Warren Buffet, currently one of the world's richest men, announced in 2006 that he was going to give away over 85% of his $40 billion fortune to charity. On top of this he persuaded Bill and Melinda Gates to do the same with their fortunes.

So on the quest towards your goal remember that money should never be the goal, the money will always come once you are doing something you love to do.

One life, live it.

For nearly 30 years I have kept a poem with me that I pulled from a magazine at the age of 12. It was to advertise Harley Davidson motorbikes. It goes as follows. I find it inspirational and take a minute now to read it and ask yourself if you are living your life the way you should be living it today. It goes as follows:

> If I had my life to live over, I'd try and make more mistakes next time
> I would relax
> I would be sillier than I have been this trip
> I know of very few things I would take seriously
> I would take more chances
> I would take more trips
> I would climb more mountains, swim more rivers and watch more sunsets
> I would eat more ice cream and less beans
> I would have more actual troubles and fewer imaginary ones.
> You see, I am one of those people who live sanely and sensibly hour after hour and day after day.
> Oh, I have had my moments and if I had to do it all over, I'd have more of them
> In fact, I'd try and have nothing else. Just moments, one after another.
> If I had to live my life over
> I would start bare-footed earlier in the spring and stay way later in the fall
> I would play hooky more

I would ride on more merry-go-rounds
I'd pick more daisies

Stress really is pointless

I bet you feel inspired after reading that poem. I bet it has made you ask yourself a few questions. Remember each day the clock is ticking down. Each day your 29,000 days are ticking down. As a student, I learnt a lot about stress: one of the most amazing facts I was told was that 75% of heart attacks and strokes are caused by stress alone. A 2009 CNN poll reveals that the number one reason for stress in most countries is money.

Stress has been called 'the silent killer' as it can lead to high blood pressure, chest pain, and an irregular heartbeat. While it is a myth that stress can turn hair grey, stress can cause hair loss. In fact, telogen effluvium (hair loss) can begin up to three months after a stressful event.

Stress alters the neurochemical makeup of the body, which can affect the maturation and release of the human egg. Stress can also cause the fallopian tubes and uterus to spasm, which can affect implantation. Stress in men can affect sperm count and motility and can cause erectile dysfunction. In fact, stress may account for 30% of all infertility problems. Stress can make acne worse. Researchers say that stress-related inflammation rather than a rise is sebum (the oily substance in skin) is to blame.

Laughing lowers stress hormones such as cortisol and epinephrine (adrenaline) and strengthens the immune system by releasing health-enhancing hormones. The stress hormone cortisol not only causes abdominal fat to accumulate, but it also enlarges individual fat cells, leading to what researchers call 'diseased' fat.

Stress is linked to the six leading causes of death: heart disease, cancer, lung ailments, accidents, liver cirrhosis and suicide. Chronic stress floods the brain with powerful hormones that are meant for short-term emergency situations. Chronic exposure can damage, shrink, and kill brain cells.

Stress makes the blood 'stickier,' in preparation for an injury. Such a reaction, however, also increases the probability of developing a blood clot. Research has shown that dark chocolate reduces stress hormones such as cortisol and other fight-flight hormones. Additionally, cocoa is rich in antioxidants called flavonoids. Stress can result in more headaches as a result of the body rerouting blood flow to other parts of the body. The hyper-arousal of the body's stress response system can lead to chronic insomnia. When cells shrink due to exposure to stress hormones, they disconnect from each other, which contributes to depression.

Stress creates hormonal changes in the human body that can decrease libido and sex response. Stress within the body affects major systems including the nervous and endocrine systems. Stress releases a chemical called cortisol, a protein fat which metabolises into glucose. The releasing of this chemical comes from messages sent to the brain when you are stressed. The 'flight or fight response' comes when the brain perceives a stressful situation (or danger) and receives a hormonal signal (in the adrenal medulla.)

The adrenal medulla reacts and releases norepinephrine

(noradrenaline) and epinephrine (adrenaline) while also sending a message to the adrenal gland (located on top of your kidneys) to release cortisol and other products.

Now all this is fine if you have to out run a lion or go into battle. But, we don't do to much of that these days, so we get stressed in traffic, on the mobile, in work, at home, watching TV, listening to the radio, on Facebook - we get stressed too much and this is damaging our immune system and overall health.

Here are my top 15 tips to reduce the stress in your life right now

1. Listen to classical music in the car, on the iPod, in the house. Stop listening to news radio all the time - it will just upset you.

2. Take hot baths with candles and relaxing music as often as possible

3. Walk daily and exercise as much as possible; a light walk of 15 minutes daily can produce great changes.

4. Cut back on coffee, tea and fizzy drinks; caffeine is not good if you need to relax.

5. Cut back on sugar, alcohol and smoking. Smokers are statistically more stressed then non-smokers, so claiming you are stressed and need to smoke is not correct.

6. Keep the same sleep pattern and try and get at least 6 to 8 hours sleep per night

7. Plan your day in advance, make a list, get your clothes ready the night before, be organised.

8. Get out in the sun for a short amount of time each day, even for a walk at lunchtime to gain vitamin D from the sun (even when it is cloudy).

9. Have a morning routine when you wake up and a night time routine before you go to bed.

10. Use your bedroom just for sleeping, no TV or radio.

11. Take time to chat to friends and family and laugh as much as you can.

12. Cut out negative activities and people from your life.

13. Eat a healthy mixed diet.

14. Focus your work day with time management.

15. Try getting a relaxation 'app' for your phone or just listen to classical music for your commute.

Change the way you see situations to reduce stress

I mentioned the advice below briefly in chapter 2. This information was e-mailed to me and I think this list of 15 things which, if you give up on them, will make your life a lot better, is well worth a read. We hold on to so many things that cause us a great deal of pain, stress and suffering. Instead of letting them all go, instead of allowing ourselves to be stress free and happy, we cling on to them. Not anymore. Starting today, you should take on the advice listed in this e-mail, it will change the way you look at life.

1. Give up your need to always be right. There are so many of us who can't stand the idea of being wrong, even at the risk of ending great relationships or causing a great deal of stress and pain, for us and for others. It's just not worth it. Whenever you feel the 'urgent' need to jump into a fight over who is right and who is wrong, like Wayne Dyer, ask yourself this question; 'Would I rather be right, or would I rather be kind?'

2. Give up your need for control. Be willing to give up your need to always control everything that happens to you and around you – situations, events, people, etc. Whether they are loved ones, co-workers, or just strangers you meet on the street – just allow them to be. Allow everything and everyone to be just as they are and you will see how much better that will make you feel.
'By letting it go it all gets done. The world is won by those who let it go. But when you try and try, the world is beyond winning' - Lao Tzu

3. Give up on blame. Give up on your need to blame others for what you have or don't have, for what you feel or don't feel. Stop giving your powers away and start taking responsibility for your life.

4. Give up your defeatist self-talk. How many people are hurting themselves because of their negative, polluted and repetitive self-defeating mindset? Don't believe everything that your mind is telling you – especially if it's negative and self-defeating. You are better than that. As Eckhart Tolle said: 'The mind is a superb instrument if used rightly. Used wrongly, however, it becomes very destructive'.

5. Give up your limiting beliefs about what you can or cannot do, about what is possible or impossible. From now on, you are no longer going to allow your limiting beliefs to keep you

stuck in the wrong place. Spread your wings and fly!
'A belief is not an idea held by the mind, it is an idea that holds the mind' - Elly Roselle

6. Give up complaining. Give up your constant need to complain about those many, many, many things – people, situations or events that make you unhappy, sad and depressed. Nobody can make you unhappy, no situation can make you sad or miserable unless you allow it to. It's not the situation that triggers those feelings in you, but how you choose to respond to it. Never underestimate the power of positive thinking.

7. Give up the luxury of criticism. Give up your need to criticise things, events or people that are different than you. We are all different, yet we are all the same. We all want to be happy, we all want to love and be loved and we all want to be understood. We are all looking for something unique in our lives.

8. Give up your need to impress others. Stop trying so hard to be something that you're not just to make others like you. It doesn't work this way. The moment you stop trying so hard to be something that you're not, the moment you take off all of your masks, the moment you accept and embrace the real you, you will then find that people will be effortlessly drawn to you.

9. Give up your resistance to change. Change is good. Change will help you move from A to B. Change will help you make improvements in your life and also the lives of those around you. Follow your bliss, embrace change – don't resist it: 'Follow your bliss and the universe will open doors for you where there were only walls' - Joseph Campbell

10. Give up labels. Stop labelling those things, people or events that you don't understand as being weird or different and try opening your mind, little by little. Minds only work when open;
'The highest form of ignorance is when you reject something you don't know anything about.' - Wayne Dyer

11. Give up on your fears. Fear is just an illusion, it doesn't exist – you created it. It's all in your mind.
'The only thing we have to fear is fear itself' - Franklin D. Roosevelt

12. Give up your excuses. Send them packing and tell them they're fired. You no longer need them. A lot of times we limit ourselves because of the many excuses we use. Instead of growing and working on improving ourselves and our lives, we get stuck, lying to ourselves, using all kind of excuses – excuses that 99.9% of the time are not even real.

13. Give up the past. I know, I know. It's hard. Especially when the past looks so much better than the present and the future looks so frightening, but you have to take into consideration the fact that the present moment is all you have and all you will ever have. The past you are now longing for – the past that you are now dreaming about – was ignored by you when it was present. Stop deluding yourself. Be present in everything you do and enjoy life. After all, life is a journey, not a destination. Have a clear vision for the future, prepare yourself, but always be present in the now.

14. Give up attachment. This is a concept that is so hard to grasp for most of us and I have to tell you that it was for me too - it still is - but it's not impossible. You get better and better at it with time and practice. The moment you detach yourself from all things, the happier you will

be. That doesn't mean that you give up your love for them, because love and attachment have nothing to do with one another. Attachment comes from a place of fear, while real and genuine love is pure, kind, and selfless. Where there is love, there cannot be fear, and because of that, attachment and love cannot coexist. With love, you become so peaceful, so tolerant, so kind, and so serene. You will get to a place where you will be able to understand all things without even trying. A state beyond words.

15. Give up living your life to other people's expectations. Too many people are living a life that is not theirs to live. They live their lives according to what others think is best for them, they live their lives according to what their parents think is best for them, what their friends, their enemies and their teachers, their government and the media think is best for them. They ignore their inner voice, that inner calling. They are so busy with pleasing everybody, with living up to other people's expectations, that they lose control over their lives. They forget what makes them happy, what they want, what they need....and eventually they forget about themselves. You have one life – this one right now – you must live it, own it, and especially don't let other people's opinions distract you from your path.

I have no idea who wrote this advice but I really admire them. Another article I came across while researching this work was written by Bronnie Ware, a palliative care worker who has worked with a countless number of patients who are sadly seeing their last days on earth.

As Bronnie questioned the patients about any regrets they had or anything they would do differently, common themes surfaced again and again in her book '*The Top 5 Regrets of the Dying*'. Here are the top 5. I must admit that I find them very moving to read:

1. I wish I'd had the courage to live a life true to myself, not the life others expected of me. This was the most common regret of all. When people realise that their life is almost over and they look back clearly on it, it is easy to see how many dreams have gone unfulfilled. Most people had not honoured even a half of their dreams and died knowing that it was due to choices they had made, or not made. It is very important to try and honour at least some of your dreams along the way. From the moment that you lose your health, it is too late. Health brings a freedom very few realise until they no longer have it.

2. I wish I hadn't worked so hard. This came from every male patient that I nursed. They missed their children's youth and their partner's companionship. Women also spoke of this regret. But as most were from an older generation, many of the female patients had not been breadwinners. All of the men I nursed deeply regretted spending so much of their lives on the treadmill of a work existence. By simplifying your lifestyle and making conscious decisions along the way, it is possible to not need the income that you think you do. And by creating more space in your life, you become happier and more open to new opportunities, ones more suited to your new lifestyle.

3. I wish I'd had the courage to express my feelings. Many people suppressed their feelings in order to keep peace with others. Many developed illnesses relating to the bitterness and resentment they carried as a result. As a result, they settled for a mediocre existence and never became who they were truly capable of becoming. We cannot control the reactions of others. Although people's initially reaction, when you change the way you are, may be to speak honestly to you, in the end it raises the relationship to a whole new and healthier level. Either that or it releases the unhealthy relationship from your life. Either way, you win.

4. I wish I had stayed in touch with my friends. Often they would not truly realise the full benefits of old friends until their dying weeks and it was not always possible to track them down. Many had become so caught up in their own lives that they had let golden friendships slip by over the years. There were many deep regrets about not giving friendships the time and effort that they deserved. Everyone misses their friends when they are dying.

It is common for anyone in a busy lifestyle to let friendships slip. But when you are faced with your approaching death, the physical details of life fall away. People want to get their financial affairs in order. But it is not money or status that holds the true importance for them. They want to get things in order more for the benefit of those they love. Usually though, they are too ill and weary to manage this task. It all comes down to love and relationships in the end. That is all that remains in the final weeks - love and relationships.

5. I wish that I had let myself be happier. This is a surprisingly common regret. Many did not realise until the end that happiness is a choice. They had been stuck in old patterns and habits. The so-called 'comfort' of familiarity overflowed into their emotions, as well as their physical lives. Fear of change had them pretending to others, and to themselves, that they were content. When deep within, they longed to laugh properly and have silliness in their life again. When you are on your deathbed, what others think of you is a long way from your mind. How wonderful to be able to let go and smile again, long before you are dying. Life is a choice. It is YOUR life. Choose consciously, choose wisely and honestly. Choose happiness.

Bronnie Ware – 'The Top 5 Regrets of the Dying'
is available at www.bronnieware.com

Chapter 6

How do we set your goals?

If you remember back to in chapter 1, I mentioned that about half of all American Presidents were either first born or only children, as were nearly all astronauts. According to the work of the neo-freudist Alfred Adler, the position you come in your family may have an outcome on the type of person you become and affect the way you live your life.

Are you the first born?

This is known in psychology as the birth order effect. Adler claimed it could be a major social determinant of personality. The first born in the family tends to get a lot of attention, discipline and has more photos taken than any subsequent child. They are positioned in a place of honour and revered by other children. This sibling rivalry and striving for superiority remains in every family, mostly in an unconscious state. Adler claimed that first born children were conscientious and conservative but can also develop feelings of insecurity and jealousy of additions to the family over time.

Are you the second born?

The second born already has someone to look up to, can be told what to do and how to do it by the first born. They look up to the first born and compete for attention and affection from parents. The second born may find it difficult to gain attention so they may use new ways to get attention from the parents, such as picking different sports or hobbies to the first born. In turn they develop different personality traits. Parenting for the second born is less restrictive so the child has more freedom. They are allowed to have more independence and create their own character. Being more able to freely express his/ her own unique personality, they may become more adventuresome, fun-loving, gregarious, maybe more creative and artistic. The second born may try to outdo the older child, they may be more rebellious and envious but they can be well adjusted. However, if a different gender than the first born, they can develop some first born traits.

Are you the third child?

This is when the theory gets complicated. The third born into a family may have more difficult challenges. They may have to create more ways to be different in order to gain power and recognition. They may not be as strongly watched or disciplined as the first two children. They will have a lot more freedom than the first two children. They will not have as much parental emphasis on becoming a high achiever.

If they family becomes bigger (more than 3 children) this may leave the 3rd child as the 'Malcolm in the Middle'. Not the oldest with the superiority, but not the youngest and the baby of the family. Middle children form alliances with others in the family, maybe the second born. The middle child may identify with the second born but be plagued by feelings of parental neglect, inadequacy and inferiority. They may therefore crave demonstrations of affection, which is a sign of insecurity. They may also have issues forming their own personality.

It is difficult for the middle child to form a power base. They tend not to feel they are loved as much as the older siblings. They strive for superiority so therefore may find a way to gain unique talents and become the child who is 'centre stage.' They may not feel as important or valued as the older siblings.

Are you the youngest child?

The fourth or youngest child tends to be a happy child that holds a coveted special place in the family, especially if there has been a gap between the first three and the fourth arrival. Parents are reluctant to let their baby grow up. The youngest may tend to be immature and irresponsible. The amount of love shown to the youngest allows him/ her to be secure, confident and happy. Rules will be most relaxed for them. They usually have the least amount of family responsibility. This will often lead to a lack of responsibility and avoidance of additional commitments as they get older.

They can develop a spontaneous, good natured personality and be very likeable with free spirits. Well know comedians and talk show hosts may often be the baby of the family. However, sometimes they can also be resentful of older siblings and have feelings of envy, jealousy and a sense of inferiority. Sometimes they refuse to grow up and become responsible as they get older.

Don't worry if you notice some traits for your position in the family that you don't like. Most experts feel that they have no real influence on personality theory. Most studies examining birth order are inconsistent.

Goal time

Throughout your lifetime, outside influences have affected who you are and what your life has become. Some, like your birth order, you have had no control over. Other reasons you have had total control over and therefore you must accept that your life up to this point has been your own doing.

Issues we have looked at over the past few chapters may have affected you and may even have stopped you living the life you wanted to live and doing what you wanted with your 29,000 days.

So now it's time to move forward. Now that we know where we have come from, we now need to look at where we are going. This involves the most important topic, which concerns your future goals.

Goals can relate to your ability to anticipate the future and be self motivated. Your goals from now on are going to help you organise your future, your behaviour and your priorities and select what's right for you going forward. The most important thing about your goals is that they are organised into a system. This system must be flexible and is influenced by the most important issues at a particular time or opportunities offered to you at that time. In other words, we need to set our goals and then allow ourselves to be flexible around situations that arise on the way to achieving these goals.

So now it's time for the master plan, your future moves. Like a chess player it's time to compose your strategy. It's time to plan your future, because without that plan, you will never reach your destination.

Organised planning to clarify your future goals is where we will start our journey. You must start with a definite goal. As mentioned earlier, the best way to do this is to sit down right now with a blank sheet of paper and start writing. What do you want from life? If you could click your fingers right now and make anything happen, what would it be?

Money?
Love?
Travel?
Health?

It does not matter as you don't need to share your goals with anyone at all. Just write them down, pretend that there are no limits to your powers and that by clicking your fingers you could have anything you wanted - what would it be?

Once you have your goal written down, you now need to plan the steps you are going to take to get to that destination. Surround yourself from now on only with positive people and with those who can help you carry out your plan. Do you need to learn new skills to reach your goal? Do you need to get certain work experience to get to your goal? Do you need the help of certain people to arrive at your goal? Then write down exactly who these people are. How are you are going to contact them, do you know anyone who can introduce you to them?

They may be leaders in the field you wish to move into, they may already have successful businesses similar to one you wish to move into, they may have already done what you wish to do. How can you get them to help you? There is one simple way to do this; just ask them. Most people are fair and normal: once you ask them for some advice or direction, 99% of people will help, if only due to the fact that someone did the same for them when they were starting out.

Next, remember to never, ever, give up on your goal. It does not matter how much disappointment you come across on your journey. You must never ever, ever give up on your goal. No person who expected to accumulate any level of success in life did so without expecting some temporary defeat along the way. Remember the old saying 'a quitter never wins and a winner never quits'.

The next step is intelligent planning of your route to success - the details of every step of the journey. Remember from now on that you are a leader, not a follower. Make that choice right now, say to yourself, I am a leader, a maverick. I do not follow those who came before me. I do not care what anyone else thinks or does, I do what I feel in my gut is the right thing to do. The followers will not get the same rewards as the leader, much like the employee will not get the same rewards as the employer - he who takes the risks gets the rewards.

Don't get me wrong, it is OK to be an intelligent follower. Most successful leaders had a mentor or someone else they looked up to, to learn from and to gain experience with. Pick your mentor, it can be someone you know or someone you have heard about. You may not have access to a leader like Donald Trump but you have access to a local businessman who is very successful. Learning from your leader before going out on your own is important.

You will need courage and faith in yourself and your own goals. This is your dream so don't expect anyone else to understand where you are coming from. You will need self-control and determination to reach your goals. You will need to be able to make fast and positive decisions to obtain your goal. You must have every step of your journey planned in advance. There should be no guess work on the road to success. Know every step of the way, therefore you will always be on the right track. Always do more than you are expected to do with each step of your journey, give everything you do 150% of your energy. It will make you stand out among the crowd.

You will need to be positive, communicate effectively, and resolve any problems at home or at work that get in the way of your goal. You will need to concentrate every day on your goals. Have a good positive personality and be focused on where you are all of the time and where you are going next. You must master the details of everything you do in order for you to be ahead of the game. You must also remember that you are now the person with full responsibility for your actions and your future.

In order for you not to fail you must have a great ability to organise your life and a willingness to be humble around others - no one likes a big headed person. People will pay you for what you do, not for what you think you can do. You must have no fear of the future, winners have no time for fear. You must use your imagination every day,

The way you currently organise your life is due to the past and experiences you have learned by watching your parents and others within your environment. This is called 'Modelling' and is part of what psychologists called Social Learning Theory. This involves processes such as attentional, retention, motor reproduction and motivational. These are the ways we learn to do things.

Who you are is a collection of habits that you have learnt from your environment. Today we need to change them. A famous psychologist called Bronfenbrenner broke down the human environment into five levels. The microsystem (family), the mesoystem (friends/extended family), the exosystem, macrosystem and chronosystem. The latter three are related to your schooling, neighbourhood, city and country etc. Parts of your personality that you learn from these systems lead you to developing something called conditioning.

Operant and classical conditioning are fancy names for habits. We do something bad and we get punished (negative reinforcement), for example driving too fast and getting a speeding ticket. This changes our behaviour. We work and we get paid; this is positive reinforcement, therefore we go back to work the next day. If we did not get paid, people would tend not to go back to work the next day. The effects of these processes have been studied for years by psychologists. The behaviour you have learned throughout your life has led you to the position you are in today and the position you wish to change.

By setting new goals, you are reconditioning your mind and making extinct your old habits. As mentioned above, if you went to work this week and didn't get paid, then you would more than likely not go back next Monday. This is called extinction.

Behaviour analysts refer to the act of extinction as extinguishing behaviour. The reinforcer (money) is simply stopped and the behaviour stops. If the reinforcement continues, the behaviour will continue. The best example of reinforcement for behaviour can be seen with gambling. Most gamblers spend their lives trying to get that big win, which got them hooked in the first place and normally happened when they gambled for the first time. Therefore, the more they win, the more reinforcement they get, so they keep trying to win. Sadly, the winning stops but by then the gambler is hooked and keeps trying to get that winning high. This is when reinforcement becomes intermittent reinforcement or addiction. The gambler is not getting the same reward but keeps trying to get it; the reward is not constant but intermittent, or rare.

A different study in the 1950s showed that in order to stop a psychiatric patient visiting the nurses' station up to 16 times a day, an extinction process was used. The visits of 16 times a day was starting to interfere with the nurses' work so psychologists told the nurses to stop paying attention to the patient. After seven weeks, visits by the patient were down to 2 per day.

Don't let your education stop you

A lot of people claim they can't do anything they want as they don't have the brains for it, they claim they can't get what they want from life as they did not go to the right school or get the right start in life. Again, this has to stop right now. You can do anything you want and how well or badly you did at school may have nothing to do with how well you do in life.

A psychologist called Gardner claims that there are seven different types of intelligence - linguistic, logical (maths), spatial, musical, bodily-kinaesthetic (things you can do with your body, like dancers), interpersonal (understanding oneself) and intrapersonal (understanding others) and naturalistic (understanding the natural world). You may think you don't have the skills to do what you want to do, but you do have the skills, you just don't know it yet.

We all have traits and some of your traits can make you a success. For example, an extrovert has talents such as being sociable, lively, active, assertive and sensational. If you are shy and don't have these traits but wish you did, here is more good news. We can change the way our brain is, to allow it to take in new experiences and benefit from them. This is called neuroplasticity, and refers to the ability of the brain to change as a result of one's experiences. The brain can change and is plastic in a way, it continues to change through-out our life span, so you are always learning and changing, the more you do, the more you experience, the smarter you get.

Research from Harvard University shows that changing your behaviour to that of a happier person can also reduce the chance that you will get a heart attack. Author and researcher Julia Boehm says: 'The absence of negative is not the same as the presence of positive. We found that factors such as optimism, life satisfaction and happiness are associated with a reduced risk of cardiovascular disease regardless of a person's age, socioeconomic status, smoking status or body weight. For example, the most optimistic individuals had approximately a 50% reduced risk of experiencing an initial cardiovascular event compared with their less optimistic peers.'

The research also showed that those who were optimistic about the future were also more likely to exercise, eat a good balanced diet and get enough sleep.

The create a better mind-body mix, some international companies have started to understand that keeping their staff happy and stress free can lead to higher productivity. Google, Yahoo, Apple, NASA and Nike all organise free meditation classes and quiet rooms so staff can escape from the noise of the work place.

Not sure what your goals are yet? Let's do some reinforcement

Let's return to your goals. You need to start planning today. Ask yourself what in your life do you want to change? Is anything distressing you? If you could snap your fingers and make your life the one you want by changing anything, what would it be?

How has your life been affected by the things that you wish to change – a bad job, bad relationship or a lack of money? Think about your day to day life, think about what you wish could be different today? Your home life, work life, social life, your body? Is your life limited due to any issues?

What thoughts accompany ideas that come into your head? In other words what stops you from making the changes you know you should make and that you want to make? Put first things first. Start with something simple, like an action plan. Not just what you want to change in your life, but how you are going to change it. Remember that from now on just thinking about the things you want to change in your life will not cut it. The days are counting down. It's all about action now.

We need to accurately define our goal. Just thinking about change will not make change happen. You mind is goal-directed, which means that once you have set that goal, your mind will go all out to get that goal for you. So setting a positive goal will help you get well on your way. You have no time for negativity anymore. That old you is gone now, the new you is going to know where you are going and furthermore how you are going to get there.

Your goal must be 'specific' for it to become a reality. I have mentioned this before. It cannot just be 'I want money', it must be 'I want a million dollars'. It cannot be 'I want a nice car', name the car you want, even get a photo of the car to remind you of the style and colour of the exact car you want. No more 'Maybe' or 'But'. That was the old you. The new you is just going to get you what you want.

You must also be able to quantify your goal. It must be tangible. It must not be flighty or something that is not real, like that you want to be a Jedi. Be realistic with your goal, it must be based in reality. Saying 'I want to be happy every day', is not really going to happen. Saying 'I want to be happier' is more realistic.

Set a time limit on the goal, this is the driver of your target. You must have a timetable so you can aim for certain points in the pursuit of your goal. This is where the plan we have talked about comes into play. The plan to get you to your goal should be broken up into two lists of things for you to do.

The first list involves immediate tasks and the second ongoing tasks. List one is the things you can do today to get closer to your goal, such as applying online for jobs, walking to lose weight, eating less junk food, joining a dating site, saving money to build a nest egg. The second list concerns ongoing tasks - long term goals like finding a new job, losing 5 stone (70lbs) in weight, finding love and a good relationship, buying a dream home.

You must also examine why you want to make these changes in your life. What is motivating you to change? Where is this change coming from? What do you need to do to motivate yourself more?

Remember the goal rules

- Your exact goals.
- The time frame you are going to get there in.

- What can you do today?
- What can you change long-term?
- Will your life be better once you have achieved these goals?
- Will you feel different once you have achieved your goals?
- What is your long-term plan?
- How will you maintain your goals and motivation?

The key to success is breaking the goals down, to do something every day that gets you closer to the goals. When a baby walks or talks he/ she does not start and get it all done in one day, they take baby steps and this is what you will do over time. Splitting the goals down into smaller goals makes the overall journey much easier over time.

You must choose the goal that you want, not the goal that someone else wants you to go for. You will change your mindset to that of someone who knows that you are going to get to your goal; it may not be today or tomorrow but it will happen. You will welcome any challenges that you face. You will find that every day you are one step closer; even when things go wrong, they are just learning experiences, educating you and helping you get one step closer to your end position.

Even if you start with one goal and then realise that you need to change your goal, that's fine. Sometimes we get on the ladder of life and get to the top before realising that we are on the wrong ladder, so we jump off and start again. That's all fine.

To obtain your goal, you must change your belief system. In

CBT (Cognitive Behavioural Therapy) they use a method called ABC on clients.

The method can be broken down into

(A) actual or activating event

(B) Beliefs and meanings about the event

(C) Emotional and behavioural consequences

For example, the A means something like, you hear that the company you work for is having financial difficulties. Therefore, before anything else has happened, you take this activating event and add your own meaning to the event (which is the B). You get upset and think you will be out of a job, on the street broke, unable to find work, living out of trash cans, homeless, with no friends and no money. You may then find yourself in a state of anxiety and stress. These are the emotional and behavioural consequences of your thought process.

The guy next to you in work hears the same news. He thinks the company is having trouble; however, even though it is the same A, his beliefs about the event lead him to think that the troubles are not serious and if they are he will get a nice payout if the company closes down (B). He has always wanted to travel and spend more time with his family; if the company closes he can do that (C). He is smart and educated and he knows he can start looking for a new job and that the future will be fine, hence his more optimistic emotional and behavioural consequence.

From now on you are going to be the second guy in that story.

Everything that happens to you happens for a reason. It's your destiny. Most things we imagine never happen. Ten people will react to the same situation in ten different ways. They will all see the event, have an emotional response from the event and assess the consequences differently. You never see things as negative anymore because those who win do not have the time or luxury for a negative thought.

Chapter 7

DON'T WORRY, BE HAPPY

Now that you have your goals written down, don't start to worry and put yourself under pressure that things will not work out. They will. The days are counting down, what's the worst that could happen. I often say to clients who are stressed about certain issues 'can it kill you?' It never can, so I then ask 'what are you killing yourself over it for?'

Always put any worries you have into perspective. Always consider the less terrifying explanations. The world is not going to end. Weigh up the evidence on the issue you are worried about. Focus on what you are doing, don't worry about the future. If you have your goals set, the future will take care of itself. Your only mission is to take 100% responsibility for your own life, set out your own goals and make an action plan. Then just follow it. A lot of people who get stressed have an all or nothing mentality. Everything is black or white for them but life is not like this.

None of us has a crystal ball and can tell the future, no one can tell you if something you do will work out or not - that's life. You can't read minds, so worrying about what others are thinking about you is a waste of time. Remember what I said earlier 'other people's opinion of you is none of your business.' Someone once told me at 20 years old you worry about what everyone thinks of you, at 40 you don't care what anyone thinks and by 60 you realise no one was thinking about you at all. But, you spend years living your life in order not to upset others.

If you do get upset by something someone says, stop and ask yourself, what am I feeling now? Ask yourself why do you care what this person thinks of the things you are doing with your 29,000 days? Take time out to think about how you will react or if you will bother to react at all. You will find that those unpleasant feelings you have in your stomach will go away very quickly, once you reason with your unconscious mind.

Stop over-generalising about life, everyone does not think you are mad to leave your job and follow your dreams. Not everyone is looking at you if you are out jogging and you look big in shorts - no one cares. Those who do care don't matter, so why should you care about them? Stop feeling sorry for yourself if something goes wrong. Dust yourself off and get back on the horse; it's all just education. Stop trying to avoid failing or making mistakes; most successful people will tell you that they only became successful by making mistakes - that's how they learnt.

Stop saying to yourself: 'I should have done this or that'. It's all a waste of time, thinking about what you could or should have done. You will find that regret in general is only waste of your time and energy. Keep an open mind from now on. The days are counting down and an open mind will help you to see things in their true perspective.

Remove yourself from the problems of the universe. Stop watching every news story on TV about disasters and shootings. Did you do any of them? NO. Then stop getting down about it. If something bad has happened, it was not your responsibility. Unless you did it. Stop toxic thoughts coming into your head. Become more objective about your thoughts.

Feelings of anger, anxiety, depression, envy, guilt, hurt, jealousy and shame are nearly always a waste of your energy. Stop avoiding things in life, don't let yourself be withdrawn from life, stop being isolated or inactive. Face every day and stop being afraid of everything and everyone. It does not matter, the days are counting down. Today – now - is the time to change. Stop putting stuff off until another day; you don't have that many left. Stop seeking reassurance from other people and just do whatever you need to do right now.

If you are doubting yourself, ask yourself simple questions about your thoughts when they become negative. Can I prove these negative thoughts to be true? What effect are these ideas having on my mind and emotions? Am I thinking logically about my situation? Do people I respect and usually agree with think that I am crazy for wanting to change my life? What evidence do I have for thinking this way? Why do I feel concern, annoyance, sadness, remorse, disappointment or sorrow right now?

Break every issue that comes up in your day into two sections. First, is this a challenging situation or a non-threatening situation? Listen to what is happening during the situation, don't jump in. Always think before you speak. Be present in the moment, stop and think. Remember that a thought is just a thought, you must have control of everything you do from now on. Focus all the time.

Become aware of everything in your life from this moment on.

Remember that the premise of this book is that we all only have a certain number of days in this life, and we all must live the life we choose. It is not just one choice that makes up your current life, but a collection of many choices you have made which has landed you where you are right now, right this moment.

The choices we all have in life are made daily, hourly, moment by moment. You must ask yourself: 'have my choices worked for me in the past and am I happy with where I am now?' Or should you try something new, and take a risk? Do you seek out adventure or continue living a life where you can predict nearly every minute of your existence?

In short, do you pursue what you want or do you simply stay on the comfortable safe road? Sadly, the majority of people live most of their lives on the safe road, the familiar road; a well-worn and well-known road. After saying no to all the new experiences, you are left with the place that you are in right now and if you are reading this book, there is a good chance that you are not too happy with that place right now and that you want to change it.

This brings us back to the comfort zone. Anything outside that zone feels uncomfortable. Most people don't like that uncomfortable feeling, the chance of failure; therefore, they never take any risks. You have heard people in the past saying: 'I don't want to do that, it makes me uncomfortable. That uncomfortable feeling is the usual reason that people don't do things in life, but you are now going to overcome those feelings and just do them anyway.

Stay happy

Having an optimistic factor within your personality may also save your life. Research from the Harvard School of Public Health has shown that those of us who are happier have a lower risk of fatal heart attacks. People who are able to enjoy simple pleasures, have a sunny disposition and a positive outlook on life are less likely to have heart attacks and strokes. It was well known that stress and depression increase the chances of being unwell and are harmful for the heart but less was known about the effect of positive emotions on health. A review by Harvard University examined 200 separate research studies which looked at psychological well-being and cardiovascular health.

Each of the 200 research papers measured the extent to which individuals consider themselves a happy or unhappy person, satisfaction with their life and the extent to which they experience pleasurable feelings. Some also looked at optimism, hope and the extent to which individuals have expectancies for positive outcomes in the future and enthusiasm for life.

Diet, you are what you eat

One of the world's fastest growing health problems is obesity. In general in the western world one in every four people is obese. Within Europe the number of cases is doubling every 10 years. Why is this an issue? Being overweight can lead to a shortened lifespan. In other words, if you are overweight and think you have 29,000 days in your life, you don't. In fact, unless you get your weight under control, you will sadly have a lot less than 29,000 days in your life.

Let's have an overview of how diet can affect you on a day to day basis. If you are overweight you will have higher than normal levels of cholesterol. Cancer is another illness which can be related to diet. Diets high in fat and low in fibre are associated with cancer. Some foods are known to increase the risk of cancer and some lower the risk. A great book to read is *Anti-Cancer a New Way of Life*, which will be wake up call for those of you worried about the illness. Another illness you need to worry about if you are overweight is Type 2 diabetes. Obesity can also result in hypertension or high blood pressure. Cutting out salt and caffeine are two ways in which you can lower your blood pressure. Being obese can also lead to joint pain and back trauma. Being overweight will also lead to psychological issues such as low self esteem and poor self image. Further down the road this may turn to depression so it is very important to examine what we can do about this issue if it affects you.

We need first to examine if everything is your fault and whether you are overweight just because you are eating too much or do not exercise enough. People do inherit their metabolism from their parents, so there may be a genetic influence. In addition, the older we get, the slower our metabolism gets, so the harder it is to lose weight. Each person may have up to 25-35 billion fat cells in their body. The number of fat cells we have in our bodies remains the same from adolescence, but the levels of fat in them is mainly due to lifestyle factors.

Another issue to look at if you are overweight is the chemical leptin. This is the chemical that is sent to your brain to let you know that you have eaten enough. Some severely obese people have a shortage of leptin, which means that they are never full.

However, some people overeat for a number of reasons, none of which are anything to do with food, which in turn leads to weight gain. These reasons include anxiety, stress, boredom, depression and relationship issues. Sometimes we eat when we are not even hungry.

So how do we lose weight? I have found that hypnotherapy plays a key role in helping people change their eating habits. More exercise and dietary change are the best ways to lose weight and once you accept this, things get a lot easier in the battle of the bulge. Some professionals recommend not watching television, no unhealthy rewards for yourself, no high cholesterol or sugary foods, eating a healthy diet and monitoring your weight monthly. A rise in TV watching and car ownership over recent years has seen more and more people moving less and eating more. We find in the clinic that losing weight and keeping weight down is difficult for a lot of people, and this leads to Yo-Yo dieting. Most people feel they can lose weight on their own but they like to have help. This is why the weight loss industry is one of the biggest in the world. Using hypnotherapy with my clients, I have found that over a month, they can lose anything from one to two stone (14-28 pounds). But, walking for an hour a day together with looking at what you eat and how you eat is essential for true weight loss. You should be able to lose 2/3 lbs per week this way and since each pound consists of 3,000-3,500 calories, that's not bad if you can keep it up.

Exercise is without a doubt the most important component in controlling weight. But, to lose weight long term you will need to focus on a multidimensional approach. This includes getting advice on nutrition and exercise, monitoring your own eating habits, motivating yourself, changing your behaviour with techniques such as hypnotherapy and not just looking at weight loss as the goal but a fitter lifestyle as the long-term aim.

Self help groups such as Weight Watchers can also help. However, we need to examine why people but on weight in the first place. You need to examine your own health behaviour to see how you can change those negative habits. In 1972 research by Belloc and Breslow found 7 behavioural changes you can make which will improve your life and health:

Sleeping 7-8 hours a day
Having breakfast every day
Not smoking
Rarely eating between meals
Being near or at your right weight
Moderate or no alcohol
Regular exercise

If you follow these rules, you are likely to reach your 29,000 days target and go even further. If people take care of themselves now, this will lead to an even greater number of people living healthily to 100 years of age in the future. It is very important to notice that how you behave now will determine your future well-being.

There are number of issues which influence your own health behaviour. These include genetic influences, which we cannot control, but also learning influences - from our parents, relatives and friends, what we eat and whether we exercise. We learn these habits by watching others. Social and environmental influences also play a part, including watching role models in sport and modern culture. Our emotional state also plays a part. The more optimistic we are, the happier we are in general.

Overall, if you want to live a good healthy life, then healthy behaviour can increase longevity. But, the likelihood that you will live a healthy life is determined by a number of factors. The most important issue when thinking about how you live your life is your own belief system, such as your readiness and willingness to change.

This will result in a much better quality of life for you during your 29,000 days. Your quality of life is not just an absence of illness but a state of complete physical, mental and social well being.

To have a good quality of life and be happy, a number of factors need to be in place. These include physical (being able to dress, wash etc.), social (having friends and social communication), emotional support (partner or family). When these are combined, you have a nice mix. You need to look not just at one aspect of your life, but at the overall landscape. There is little point going out trying to make a fortune or become famous, slim or be working at your dream job if you are not healthy enough to enjoy it and be around in the future.

Here are some interesting facts I bet you did not know about your health.

Even though women are less likely than men to have heart attacks, they are more likely to die from them if they have them. Your age, family history and educational status can also have an effect on your health and life span.

One in four deaths from heart disease is caused by smoking alone. In addition, stopping smoking can halve the risk of having another heart attack for those who have already had one. Diet is the most important issue in relation to cholesterol levels, which has been implicated in the onset of chronic heart disease.

Men with severe angina can reduce chest pain by taking part in a stress reduction programme of any kind. Men with this condition who did some physical exercise and stress management recovered much better than those who just did stress management. Stress management techniques such as progressive muscle relaxation were effective in reducing blood cholesterol levels and blood pressure in men with a Type A personality.

People who take their partners to group physical activities were less stressed then those who went alone. There is also psychological proof that exercising with a group can lower stress and anxiety levels.

Obesity levels are different worldwide. Someone who is seen as overweight in India may not be in the USA. Body mass index (BMI) is a method of measuring body fat in adults based on height and weight. A rough guide to BMI levels follows but it is advisable to get your BMI checked by a healthcare professional.

Underweight	less than 18.5
Normal weight	18.5-24.9
Overweight, grade 1	25-29.9
Clinically obesity, grade 2	30-39.9
Severe obesity, grade 3	40+

Overall obesity is greater in men than in women, Salt (sodium chloride) affects blood pressure; consuming more sodium increases blood pressure and can affect stress levels. In a study over 19 years, it was shown that caffeine can also affect your lifespan. Men who consumed more than 6 coffees per day had much higher rates of mortality due to chronic heart disease.

Diets that are high in fat and low in fibre are associated with the development of cancer of the colon and prostate gland. Some foods, including meats such as bacon and ham, increase the risk of cancer. Some foods, such as fruits, certain vegetables and high fibre breads and cereals, can reduce the risk. Overweight people tend to have some psychological issues due to pressure to conform to the stereotypical attractive image.

Psychological advances are now being used to try to change people's views on their health for the better. The major causes of death in Europe are chronic heart disease and cancer, both of which can be reduced with a change in lifestyle and behaviour. Psychological researchers are now aiming to prevent illness rather than simply cure it. This is based on what psychologists called the BioPsychoSocial model.

CBT the new black

The current trend within the field of psychology is to change behaviour using CBT (Cognitive Behavioural Therapy) or REBT (Rational Emotive Behaviour Therapy). To give you an idea of how this works, we must first look at a negative emotion. Take anxiety. This is when we think that bad things are going to happen, but that they must not happen – 'If the thing did happen I would be a bad and a worthless person'. However, the aim of this therapy is to change the approach to 'I wish it does not happen but I accept that it may happen. If it does happen, that would be bad but not awful. I wish and hope it does not happen but I accept that it can and if it does, it does not prove that I am less of a person, only that I am human'.

This type of therapy can get you to change the way you look at situations. It gets you to change feelings of anger, guilt, hurt or shame to feelings of acceptance. I would always like to do the right thing but sometimes I don't, I am only human. Or I really want to be treated fairly but I accept that some people are just not going to do that and I have to accept that. Or I want others to think of me in a good way but this may not happen and I have to accept this; it's just their opinion and it is not a fact.

Chapter 8

100 USEFUL FACTS ABOUT YOUR PSYCHOLOGY

In a recent psychological experiment, 100 participants were given two different sized bowls of ice-cream to eat. 50 were given a small bowl and 50 a large bowl. 'They were told to eat as much ice-cream as they wanted. The end result was that those with the large bowl ate nearly 50% more ice-cream than those with the small bowl who were tricked by their brain that once the small bowl was empty they were full. Therefore a good way to lose weight is to eat off a smaller plate or bowl.

This is just one example of how psychology can help in every day matters such as weight loss. Now that you have your goals set, you have a good idea of what you are going to do with your remaining days as you count down from 29,000. We are now going to examine your personality and how your personality can allow you to have the life you want, once you understand it better.

In this chapter you are going to become student psychologists. Psychology is the study of mind and behaviour. Most people have heard of Sigmund Freud, the father of modern psychology. But, psychology has been around for a lot longer than the past 100 years.

There are a number of schools of psychology - behaviourism, social learning theory, psychoanalytic theory, psychosocial theory, cognitive development theory, socio-cultural theory and many more.

In psychology, it is believed that development starts even before you are born. In the prenatal stage and the neonatal stage, teratogens - chemicals found in food, alcohol, cigarettes and the environment - can all effect the development of the unborn baby.

Behaviourism focuses on the importance of past experiences in guiding development. People learn from experience. This is based on a theory called the law of effect - actions that result in rewards or punishments. This can be called learning in some cases but only when it involves a permanent change in behaviour. This concept of learning by trial and accidental success is favoured once the outcome is favourable to the participant. This was first seen in an experiment by psychologist Edward Thorndike, who put a hungry cat in a box. To escape from the box and eat the food that was sitting outside the box, the cat had to push a latch. The cat would accidentally bump the latch and the door out to the food would open; it was found the more this was done, the shorter the time it took for the cat to open the door. This is known as gradual learning. This can also been seen with a number of experiments with monkeys.

Learning occurs as a result of your experiences in the environment that shape your behaviour. The laws of behaviourism state that learning depends on the relationship between stimulus and response. This relates more to nurture than nature when it comes to learning.

The person you are today is actually passive in your own development. Your learning over the years is gradual and continuous over your entire lifespan. Most of which you are not aware you are doing.

The school of behaviourism in psychology is best known through the work of B. F. Skinner, who showed by using a process called Operant Conditioning that you could change the way people behave. This is based on a system of positive and negative rewards for behaviour. In other words, if you get a speeding ticket on a road, the next time you drive down that road you automatically slow down to avoid the negative speeding ticket again.

An example of positive reinforcement is something that most people do everyday - going to work and getting paid. This is positive reinforcement in operation. If you went to work and did not get paid, then this reinforcement would become extinct. Operant conditioning can also be strengthened in a number of ways and it can also be decreased. This system is used globally in prisons to ensure that prisoners behave themselves. Those who are well behaved get tokens for the prison shop and are allowed extra privileges. Those who don't behave get privileges taken away from them.

There is a second type of conditioning which is important to understand when it comes to your behaviour and how you can change it. This is called classical conditioning. Operant conditioning is voluntary but classical conditioning is automatic. It is a reflex response and is repeated by both animals and humans when an appropriate stimulus is introduced. It can be seen that new stimuli can come to be associated with certain behavioural responses.

In a famous experiment in the 1890s, Ivan Pavlov discovered that by giving a dog food and ringing a bell at the same time, the dog would salivate. However, after a while, if he just rang the bell, the dog would automatically salivate even when no food was presented to him. This can seen in the ways that children are taught in school. If they are good they get treats and attention, if they are bold they get put in the naughty corner.

Taste aversion is a form of classical conditioning and is used in treating people with alcohol problems. After this process takes place, and participants have been made ill through alcohol, those who just smell alcohol automatically feel ill.

This type of treatment was also performed by John Watson on a subject called Little Albert, where a child was able to play with a white rabbit. A loud noise was introduced every time the child touched the rabbit, so the child stopped touching the rabbit and got very upset when he saw it, as he was afraid of the loud noise. A response can therefore be extinguished by simply stopping the delivery of the reinforcement. Psychological research shows that this works for children's tantrums but the punishment or withdrawal of privileges must be immediate.

The four rules for changing behaviour using reinforcement are as follows - you must deliver a reinforcer contingent on the behaviour; you must deliver it immediately; the size of the punishment must be correct, appropriate for the crime and the person must be deprived of the reinforcer.

This leads us onto another everyday issue, gambling. This is a hard habit to break as it is based on another type of reinforcement called intermittent reinforcement. Unlike continuous reinforcement, where every response is reinforced, intermittent reinforcement does not provide a constant reward for activity. Intermittent reinforcement rewards differently and it is the basis for an addiction to gambling. This can be in the form of ratio schedules, where a number of set responses is required (such as a payout every 50 pulls of the one armed bandit), interval schedules (where a specific time scale are required before payout), variable radio responses, which only pays out an average amount of times over a set time period and variable interval responses, where the response rates vary over an longer average time span - a certain amount of times in a 24 hour period but with no set timetable. It is important to note that each of the four schedules generate a different characteristic pattern of responding.

According to behaviourists 'the child is born empty into a world of coherently organised content. Like a mirror however, the child comes to reflect his environment'. Social Learning theory suggests that we learn from watching others and this is called modelling or vicarious reinforcement. John Bowlby, a psychologist, developed a theory on attachment based on children and mothers - the videos are available online. This theory tested the bond between the mother and child. He assumed that the attachments we make in childhood, which are called vertical attachments, will pattern our later horizontal relationships, which are the ones we have as adults.

Attachment is defined as relationships you have with people that are ongoing and involve emotional bonds, or as one psychologist put it: 'a long enduring, emotionally meaningful tie to a particular individual'. Attachments are very important because if we lack them, this could lead to negative consequences. This in turn could lead to a person needing psychological help further down the road of life, which will affect not just the person's relationships but also other aspects of their life, like work. Attachment is an essential part of development.

From birth, infants are completely dependent on others for care. Bowlby claimed in 1969 that infants were biologically predisposed to attach to their mother but that this is a slow and gradual process. Attachment styles will influence our behaviour towards others throughout our lives and our long term relationships. Successful attachment is vital for positive social and emotional development. Our attachment develops from 0 to 3 months as indiscriminate responsiveness to humans, and by 3 to 6 months we can focus on familiar people.

From 6 months to 2 years we have an intense attachment to parents and siblings and actively seek proximity to close family - especially the mother. Then from age 2 until the end of childhood, we have a full partnership with those we become close to. In the first 6 to 24 months, the mother is the secure base from which, as children we will not stray too far, knowing that we can always return to the safety of her arms at any time. This is fine once the mother is available and reliable as a source of comfort and security.

However, if she is not available, this can lead to negative changes in the child's development. This period has been shown to be a critical period in the development of a child, through neuroscience and cognitive psychology research with primates.

To test the bond with mothers and children, psychologist Mary Ainsworth developed an experiment called the 'strange situation', in which the mother and a stranger alternately enter and leave the room that the infant is in. The experiment is available on YouTube. Overall, the strength of an attachment in childhood can determine our future relationships as we see this as a template for how others will behave towards us as we get older.

Another aspect of social learning theory is put forward by psychologist Albert Bandura, who felt that modern learning is based only on modelling - learning that occurs by virtue of witnessing another person perform a behaviour. This could be seen in a positive way - if you see someone donating blood you may also do the same, or in a negative way if you see someone taking drugs, smoking, drinking alcohol or taking extreme risks. Bandura claimed that development is guided by observational learning and that people have the ability to regulate their own behaviour, a trait known as self-regulation. This involves using our mind and brain (cognitive factors) and it also assumes that we all have our own individual differences. The theory claims that we only learn and acquire new behaviours by observing, reading or hearing about other people's behaviour. This allows us to develop anticipated consequences. We watch those around us and develop our habits from watching them. We often copy people we feel are admirable, powerful, nurturing or similar to ourselves, like parents, friends, celebrities or successful people in society.

There are also difference types of social learning. The first is imposed, like prison, where you have no choice. The second is selected, like college or school, where you choose to stay. The third is created and based on behaviour like watching television, which leads to exposure to different models. Modelling can also lead to negative behaviour being picked up by children; this has been seen a lot recently with kids playing video games and psychological research has shown that those who play violent video games see violence in a more acceptable way.

Bandura's most famous experiment was one called the 'Bobo doll' experiment and was based on children being rewarded or punished for certain behaviour. This experiment is also available online. An adult would either play with a doll or be violent towards it, while the children looked on. Behaviour was influenced by watching an adult and results showed that boys were more easily influenced than girls, but that girls tend to follow set rules better than boys. However, when the kids were asked to repeat their actions by hitting the Bobo doll again for a reward, they still did the same as before, which means that watching an adult hitting the doll was a more powerful model than the reinforcement of a reward for non-aggressive behaviour. This was shown later to be an important experiment when examining whether watching violence on television affected children's behaviour.

Bandura finally tried out modelling of aggression by testing children with four different types of violence to see which one they copied the most. The first was getting children to watch an adult being aggressive in real life, the second was watching the adult on film, the third was watching a cartoon character performing the actions and then finally he had a control group who watched nothing.The highest level of aggression in children was found in children watching the real-life model, an adult being aggressive. No difference was found between the film and cartoon. It showed that actions, not words, have the most effect on the development of a child.

So how will all this information help you? Well some practical implications are that research has shown that spanking children increases aggressive behaviour (Bandura and Walters, 1963) and that children prefer to follow a good example without being forced to do so (White, 1972). It also found that that observational learning may reduce phobias, which Bandura showed in his 1967 experiment of children who were afraid of dogs. Finally, it showed that children who learnt from fellow students learnt better and that what the media tell us to do, or how to look or behave also has an effect on how we behave.

Sigmund Freud developed a school based on psychoanalytic theory which is still controversial. It is based on four stages - the oral, anal, phallic and genital stage plus a latent period. Freud felt that everything that happens to us in the first four years of our life affects how we behave as adults and he also related everything down to sexuality and the unconscious. It is also worth noting that behaviourism ignores the unconscious. Freud also claimed that humans have three erogenous zones (the mouth, anus and genitals) and that frustration occurs when needs are not met. If needs are always met this can lead to human indulgence. If a person gets stuck at one stage they may become fixated at this stage, hence statements like 'he is so anally retentive'.

Those who are stuck in the oral stage tend to be either having frustration at this stage and a lack of care by the mother or primary caregiver can lead to pessimism, envy, suspicion and sarcasm in later life. Those who are overindulged at this stage may be optimistic, gullible or full of admiration for others around them. Those who are stuck in the anal stage may be either someone who needs instant gratification or at the other end of the scale those who hold back for delayed gratification - those who are generous versus those who are tight fisted and mean, or those who are gregarious and those who are secretive. However, personality traits may be messy and disorganised.

If you have children, you may be interested in the work of Piaget, who saw children as little scientists. His view was that children learnt and developed in an active way over four stages. Between 0-2 years they learn by sensory and motor learning. Between 2-7 years they go through a pre-operational stage, between 7-11 years they are learning in a concrete operational way and from 12 years of age, they have a formal structured operational level of development.

So you are probably asking yourself what all of this has to do with you and your remaining 29,000 days? Well, unless we know why we are the way we are, we cannot change the things we need to change. This is what we examine in the next chapter.

Chapter 9

WHY YOU ARE THE WAY YOU ARE TODAY?

Your past behaviour can also determine how many of your 29,000 days you will have left to live and whether you will live for more or less than this. Did you know that 65% of cancer deaths are attributable to lifestyle habits with 30% due to smoking, 30% to poor diet and obesity and 5% due to lack of exercise (Willet, 1996). Did you also know that with every extra year of marriage, divorce becomes less likely? Did you know that your behaviour now will determine what type of older person you become?

There are three types of older person - the young-old, who is healthy and vigorous, financially secure, active in family and community life, the old-old, who have major physical, mental or social losses but still have some strengths and the oldest-old, who are dependent on others for almost everything. The good news is that 75% of older adults report that they are in good health. Physical problems such as hypertension and arthritis tend to be chronic and long-term but the most important factors are psychological and lifestyle related - a sense of control and optimism for life. Getting old is a little like comparing the human body to a car. If you put the wrong type of fuel in, don't take care of it, don't service it and don't exercise it, it will get sick and die on you.

Some other interesting facts about how many of the 29,000 days you will live, or if you will live more than 29,000 days. Women who were never pregnant live longer (Finch, 2000) and overweight people tend to sicken and die younger. Our brains change as we age and our working memory becomes smaller (Briggs, 1998). It also becomes harder to multi-task and focus. However, our long-term memory can improve over time and expertise is what older generations have to offer the rest of the world, although some source amnesia is common (Cralk, 2000).

Older adults have difficulty in gathering and considering all data relevant to logical analysis and decision making (Zwahr, 1999). When we get older our brain does slow down, but thinking that does not involve speed is less affected. Older people tend to refuse to guess and can be a little resistant to change. Older people tend to use tricks to remember things such as using written reminders, allowing more time to do things, taking more time to read instructions. However, just because they are older, this does not mean that they are less accurate with information than younger people.

So what can you do to help yourself in old age? To avoid conditions like dementia, hypertension, diabetes and many more illnesses, a few simple things can help. Lifestyle habits can help. Cut out poor eating and smoking and start exercising. The good thing about getting older is that you gain broad, practical and comprehensive wisdom, which gives a great insight into problems, reflecting timeless truths about life. Expertise in life will also give you exceptional insight and judgement in complex and uncertain matters.

Beware of retirement and try in older age to ensure that you keep busy. There are five stages to retirement and none sound good. They are the honeymoon stage, the disenchantment stage, reorientation, retirement routine and then termination, which means that your 29,000 days are up. The key to living longer is keeping active - use it or lose it. Continue your education and keep learning. Do volunteer work. If you wish, turn to religion and make sure that you have social support.

Throughout your life, it is important to have what we call 'homeostasis' - balance to your life, mind and body. Until we are 30 years of age our physical strength increases but from then on, we all go downhill slowly. However, whatever stage of live you are at, there are some keys to staying healthy and happy. Living life to the fullest requires you to have a flexible perspective and to think of a few different solutions to any issue that comes up. Education can also have an effect on how long you live. Those with more education have higher verbal and quantitative skills, including specific subject knowledge, enhanced reasoning, reflection and flexibility of thought.

As we live and grow, our needs change. According to Freud, as we move into adulthood our main needs are related to love. Maslow (1968) claimed that, once basic needs are met, a focus on love and belonging comes into our minds. This is followed by success, self esteem and self-actualisation.

Some psychologists, including Erikson, claim that most of us move through certain stages during life. In our 20's, we finish our education and establish our identity. By the 30's, we have found love, a house and children, bringing intimacy. Then as we go into our 40's we devote ourselves to climbing the career ladder and growing with the family. Erikson also notes that a lack of relationships for any of us leads to social isolation. But, this all depends on our gender. Men share more activities and interests with each other, while women are more intimate and emotional, providing practical assistance to each other. Female to female friendships reduce loneliness and self absorption. Male to male relationships and friendships function better in work situations.

This brings us to the subject of finding a mate. Or looking for love? Sternberg (1988) clams that there are three dimensions to love - passion, intimacy and commitment - which give rise to seven forms of love, found in all types of love, between all types of couples. These are liking love - intimacy; romantic love - passion and intimacy; infatuation – passion; fatuous love - passion and commitment; empty love – commitment; companionship love - intimacy and commitment; and consummate love - intimacy, passion and commitment. According to Armato (2003), the success of a marriage comes from the maturity of partners but intimacy is hard to develop until we have our own identity secured. Similarity is often very important to a successful relationship and major compromises are often required.

Economic downturns can be an issue which will test a relationship. When we work, we have a chance to develop and use personal skills. We can express our unique creative energy and aid and advise co-workers as a mentor or friend. We can also contribute to the larger community via our products and services. This raises the subject of women in the workplace. Did you know that since more women are working, there have been changes in the rates of marriage around the world? In Japan this has seen a reduction in the amount of weddings. In the USA, the fact that more women are working has led to an increase in the success rates of marriage. Similarly, in Sweden the chances of a marriage succeeding significantly improve if a woman works.

This also affects divorce rates, as we known the children of divorced parents may develop differently to those of more stable marriages. This may be related to stress, which has a variety of effects. Girls of divorced parents experienced puberty earlier in New Zealand (Moffitt, 1992). Polish teenagers living in crowded cities, which led to them having a more stressful lifestyle, matured faster than rural contemporaries (Halanicka, 1999). According to research by Ellis (2000), two factors influenced puberty - conflicted relationships within the family and an unrelated man living in the home (stepfather etc). Did you know that girls who hit puberty at different stages can have a different mindset to each other?

Early maturing girls may have lower self-esteem, more depression and poorer body image. They may feel isolated from peers. Many even turn to older boys for romantic relationships. Today is it is also common for puberty to occur earlier and marriage later than in the past. This may also lead to experimentation not just with sexual activity, but also with drugs and alcohol. Kids see drugs, smoking and alcohol as means to making friends.

Girls smoke to decrease their appetite. Anyone with teenagers also knows they think differently to adults. They suffer from egocentrism. This is an invincibility fable, which makes them think that they are immune to laws, mortality and probability and they therefore take more risks. They also suffer from a personal fable, as they imagine their own lives as mythical or heroic, some seeing themselves as destined for fame and fortune. Some may have an imaginary audience and are preoccupied with how others will react to them; they are not at ease with the social world around them. They tend to just think about possibilities and not practicalities. They do not see the consequences of risk taking, not worrying that some choices have long lasting effects with some adolescents overrating the joys of the moment and ignoring the future costs.

It is natural for boys to take more risks then girls. Teachers also play a significant role in how children develop. Higher teacher expectations tend to increase student interest and aspirations (Wentzel, 2002). The best teachers push students to do well and they make it easier for them to understand difficult subject matter (Tatar, 1998).

Students must believe that learning is a result of effort and not an inborn trait. A universal trait of adolescence is identity and most reconsider the goals and values set by parents and culture. The status of identity is closely linked to self esteem. Did you know that depression levels double to 15% during puberty? Hormones change, stress relating to peers, school, sexual drives and identity all become issues in teenagers' lives? In young men between 15 and 27, there is a higher rate of suicide then any other age bracket. Many adolescents become detached from their parents.

There is conflict between early maturing daughters and mothers about lifestyle and adjustment is needed on both sides. As mentioned earlier, there is significant research that shows that boys and some girls who pay violent video games will display more aggressive behaviour. Exposure to these games also makes children and young adults more psychologically aroused and aggressive, with violent thoughts and feelings. Playing violent video games also decreases pro-social behaviour (Anderson and Bushman, 2001). All these elements can come under one banner - personality traits, where do you get them from and what makes you different to the person next to you?

Traits are defined as consistent patterns in the way we behave, feel and think. They are aspects of our personality that are enduring, typical and public. Our traits help us in three main ways - to summarise, to predict and to explain how we react to situations in our lives.

They are the fundamental building blocks of your personality. These traits may cover your sociability, lively nature, activity, assertion and the sensations you feel. Your personality is very complex. Originally psychologists found 2 superfactors in personality - extroversion and introversion - the person who is active, outgoing and sociable compared to the person who is shy, quiet and unsociable. How much of each you are comes from a cocktail of events that have happened so far in your life and are happening each day, so each day you change. They can also be linked to health and links have been found between personality and illnesses such as cancer and heart disease.

One of the most famous personality models is the five factor model (Costa & McCrae, 1985). This model claims that we are made up of five different traits - each of different measures. They are openness, conscientiousness, extroversion, agreeableness and neuroticism. They are known in psychological circles as the 'big five'.

Personality and traits are totally different to intelligence. The most common themes relating to intelligence are an adaptation to the environment one is in, your basic mental processes and your reasoning or higher-order thinking. Your problem solving and decisions making skills also make up part of your intelligence. The definition of intelligence is an ability to understand complex ideas, to adapt effectively to the environment, to learn from experience, to engage in various forms of reasoning and to overcome obstacles by thinking.

This brings us to understanding more about the biological foundations for your personality. According to Sheldon, your body shape may determine certain personality characteristics. The first is the endomorph type which loves physical comfort, eating, is amiable, complacent and needs people when they are in trouble. The body shape of these people we would call cuddly or big boned, they may also come under the heading of a Type C personality. The second type is the mesomorph, who is assertive, loves physical adventure, is energetic, dominant, loves power and taking risks and is competitive. This person appears physically healthier and has a Type A personality. The last type is the ectomorph, who loves privacy, has fast reactions, emotional restraint, is sensitive to pain/chronic fatigue, and is apprehensive and self conscious; the tall, thin, awkward type.

This again brings us back to love and the picking of a mate. How you look determines who you mate with but this varies depending on your gender. Before you get upset and call men shallow and women gold diggers, evolution has a lot to do with the search for a mate. The male prefers a good looking female, because to him she has reproductive capacity, youth and physical attractiveness, but also chastity. The female seeks someone who can provide resources for her and her offspring through earning capacity, ambition and industriousness. Supermodels and millionaires are the best examples of each.

What is interesting about our views on relationships is that men are more jealous about sexual infidelity, while females are more concerned about emotional attachments and loss of resources. This is neither one's fault but it is in our DNA.

Left and right brained?

This brings us to the neuroscience and people who claim to be left brained and right brained. This is technically known as left and right hemispheric dominance. Mood disorders can also be affected by these variations, with a decreased left-anterior cortical activity linked with current and past depression (Allen, 1993). In children, those with more activation in the right hand side of the brain are more inhibited than those with more activation in the left hand side, who show a more uninhibited temperament (Kagan, 1988).

What makes you happy?

You are happy when a chemical called dopamine is released in your brain; this is central to the functioning of the rewards system and gives you a feel good response. Serotonin is also involved in mood regulation. Drugs such as Selective Serotonin Reuptake Inhibitors (SSRI) can prolong the action of serotonin at the synapse and are used in treating depression.

What do we need to be happy? One reason is a need for positive regard, to seek warmth, liking, respect, sympathy and acceptance from those around us. If we get unconditional positive regard, this fosters our own levels of higher self esteem.

If you are in a job that you hate and using up some of your 29,000 days, maybe it is time to consider the effects it is having on your health? You can be stressed in work by either working too much or too little. Those who work too much have a heavy workload and this occurs when a job requires successive speed, output or concentration. At the other end of the scale is underutilisation which happens when workers feel that their knowledge, skills or energy are not being fully used.

The main reasons for work stress are as follows: job ambiguity - from a lack of clearly defined tasks, lack of control or a feeling of having little input or effect on the job and/or work environment; the physical working conditions of the job - extreme temperatures, loud/distracting noises, crowding, poor lighting and ventilation; interpersonal stress - dealing with co-workers, customers and supervisors in the work place. Other major causes of worker stress include emotional labour - regulating and controlling emotions in the workplace, harassment, organisational change and work-family conflict.

Even worse than job stress is job loss which can result in depression, anxiety, alcohol and drug abuse and poor family relations. Stress can even affect those who are kept on in jobs where others have been let go. Issues such as job insecurity, workload stress, loss of social relations and friends can affect those left behind.

Some people you work with may have a Type A personality, which is characterised by excessive drive, competitiveness, impatience and hostility. Research has shown that those who are stressed in the workplace perform more poorly, have higher absenteeism and change jobs more often (Bhagat, 1983).

The effect this stress can have on your body and how long you live is also apparent. These include having high blood pressure, higher heart rate and higher cholesterol. Those who are stressed also suffer from illnesses such as ulcers, colitis, heart disease, migraine and headaches. Stress can also result in common colds and infections.

Motivation in the workplace sometimes comes from a need for

achievement, power or affiliation with a company or people in the company. Motivation within the job comes from responsibility, achievement, recognition of the work you do, advancement and growth of personality on the job. The elements that can lead to job dissatisfaction include company policy and administration, supervision, interpersonal relations, working conditions and salary.

So if you are wasting some of your 29,000 days in a job you hate, it may not just be boring but it may actually be doing you long term damage. Make that plan and start working towards a new job, new career or new college course to help you find a way of earning an income which does not end up killing you slowly.

Chapter 10

Stress, the silent killer

So what is stress and why do we let it control us so much. In earlier chapters, I wrote about the 'flight or fight' response. Stress comes in many ways and it is interesting to know that 75% of heart attacks and strokes are at least partly caused by stress. The definition of stress is the negative emotional experience accompanied by predictable, biochemical, physiological, cognitive and behavioural changes that are directed either towards altering the stressful event or accommodating its effects. The way we react to stress can have an effect on the amount of days we to live; in other words, unless we learn to manage our stress we will have a lot less than 29,000 days.

An issue with stress that most of us have is telling the difference between major and everyday events. What events are part of our daily lives and what do we blow out of proportion? How we see stress depends not just on our personality but also our culture, gender, race and educational background.

We all have different sources of stress - it may be illness, money, pain or conflict with someone else. Sources may come from family - divorce, illness/ death etc. - or within the community through issues such as occupational stress. There may also be environmental stress which we get from overcrowding, noise, exposure to waste or even natural disasters.

As discussed in the previous chapter, occupational stress can be a major issue and has a major effect on your health. The type of job you have, the job pressure, the responsibility, any conflicts, the physical environment, the control you have within the job, your interpersonal and social relationships, if you have an inadequate career development or any job insecurity and, of course, the possibility of unemployment, can all affect your stress levels in both the short and long term.

Occupational stress has been related to psychological distress and negative health outcomes (Regicki, 1985). The financial burden of stress within the workplace is also high due to the cost to the government of disability payments. Stress on your body and mind affects both your nervous and endocrine systems. When you get stressed, the first thing that happens to your body is that it goes into the alarm phase, then the resistance phase and then ends with the exhaustion phase. Your body feels fear and this releases adrenaline. The difference in how you react and how someone else does is all down to two fundamental concepts, your evaluation of the stress or your appraisal (am I in danger or not?), followed by your management or coping of the situation?

How can you can deal with this stress more effectively? Some basic rules are to focus on the issue at hand, have emotional support, improve your own personal control of situations, be more organised, employ better time management, exercise more, and if you know something stressful may happen be prepared for it.

Most people deal with stress in two different ways. The first is problem focused, with direct action, doing something constructive. The second is emotionally focused, which allows us to regulate our emotions to deal with the situation. There are of course many other ways to deal with stress. Some people turn to religion, some to acceptance of change, some to alcohol or drugs, some to humour and some even to denial of an event happening.

The main source of stress is money worries, followed by time pressures, low education level, a need for a good job and family pressures,. These can be offset by the presence of positive life events and a positive attitude. Did you know that individuals with greater resources cope better with stress? The better educated you are, the more skills you have acquired and the more stress management practice you have, the better you can deal with anything that comes your way.

Lifestyle choices can affect the levels of stress that you have to deal with on a daily basis. Those who smoke and drink are more stressed than those who do not. Yes, smokers are more stressed then non-smokers, so a smoker claiming that they need a cigarette to relax is only stressing themselves out more. Work-related pressures can also affect stress levels.

Research also claims that negativity can lead to poor health (Friedman, 1987) and elevated cortisol levels (Van Eck, 1996). Negativity can also create an impression of poor health when none exists (Cohen, 1995). As mentioned earlier, your personality type can also affect your health status and how long you live. Type A personalities are prone to heart attacks, with high reactivity levels, higher alcohol consumption and they are more likely to smoke. They also tend to drive themselves too hard. Another main cause of stress in everyone is having a lack of control over a situation.

Chapter 11

CREATING YOUR BUCKET LIST

You have made the choice to change your life. You have made the list of changes you wish to make. However, if you are having trouble putting you list of life changing goals together, here are some suggestions for your bucket list. A bucket list is a list of things you want to do before you 'kick the bucket'. Some are related to travel, some to sport and some to just pure old fashioned fun.

Remember your 29,000 days are counting down. I have shown you how your mind works, how you need to visualise how you want to see yourself in the future (press that left finger and thumb together again for me). You have a choice to make now, it's time to banish the fear which has stopped you, no more excuses. Get up and get that piece of paper, it's time to move, time to change. The old you has gone, the new you is the one that does things, the one who says yes. You have read everything you need to know about mind, you have become a student of psychology, you know what you have to do. Read below some of the goals you can set for yourself if you have not already done so. It's time to change, remember the mantra 'do it now' as tomorrow is promised to no one. Let's now look at a full list of goals you can add to your bucket list, life list or goal list. Hopefully it will inspire you to get planning to make the most out of your remaining 29,000 days.

Let's start with fitness. Some of the goals you can set for yourself in relation to your fitness include doing a 5k or 10k run. Running a half-marathon or even completing a marathon. You could make a trip and run the Boston Marathon, the Honolulu Marathon or the London marathon. In America some people join the 50 States Marathon Club and run a marathon in all 50 states.

You could try take part in a triathlon (participate in endurance events consisting of swimming, cycling, and running). You could take part and complete the Ironman Triathlon. You could walk across the Simpson Desert in Australia. You could complete an American Cancer Society Making Strides against Breast Cancer walk. Hike the Appalachian Trail. Learn to ride a bike efficiently and safely. Bike through National Geographic's 10 Best Bike Trails in the World.

Take a bike tour through wine country. Ride a unicycle. Go mountain biking or enter a bike race.

Participate in a stage of the Tour de France. Ride a bicycle from Los Angeles to New York. Learn to rollerblade. Learn to ride a skateboard and to do a 'wheelie' and other tricks on your skateboard. Learn to skateboard on ramps.

If you have an interest in water sports you could learn to canoe or start kayaking or sailing. Participate in a regatta (boat race) learn to windsurf.. Drive a speedboat. Ride a jet ski. Go water skiing – maybe barefoot. Ride an ice boat.

If you have always wanted to do something musical you could learn to play the piano. Take singing lessons. Learn to play the guitar. Learn to yodel. Compose a song. Release an album. Join the church choir. Learn to sing opera. Play in an orchestra. Conduct an orchestra. Form a band. Enrol in a music appreciation class. Sing Karaoke. Build a Jazz library. Build a classical music library.

You could learn to dance the Salsa, the Rumba or the Cha-cha-cha.

You could put something wild and interesting on your bucket list such as riding in a hot air balloon.

Paragliding, parasailing in Acapulco, skydiving, taking a helicopter ride, scuba diving, snorkelling in a shipwreck, swimming with sharks, riding a mechanical bull. You could climb Mount Kilimanjaro or Mount Everest, go fire walking or bungee jumping. You could go white water rafting, live in a submarine. Go rock climbing, learn to fly a plane, race a sports car, fire a pistol or go jet skiing.

You could ride the world's largest Ferris Wheels or ride the 10 largest roller coasters in the world.

You could take a cruise or visit the wreckage of the Titanic aboard a submarine. Soon enough you will be able to travel to into space with Virgin Galactic and experience weightlessness. You could go on the world's top ten train rides or watch a rocket launch, live. Why not aim to break a Guinness World Record or go on a cross-country motorcycle trip? You could jump from a cliff into deep water or swim in the world 's largest swimming pool, off the coast of Chile.

You could visit some of the world's best festivals. These include The National Cherry Blossom Festival, Washington, DC. The

Loy Krathong, the sky lantern festival in Thailand. Oktoberfest, Munich. The Brazilian Carnival, Rio de Janeiro. The Mardi Gras, New Orleans. The Ati-Atihan Festival, the Philippines. The Day of the Dead, Mexico or the Galway International Oyster Festival in Ireland. You could visit the Carnival in Venice, Italy, the Burning Man in the Black Rock Desert of Nevada or the famous La Tomatina in Valencia.

Or visit some of the world most famous natural sites including the Grand Canyon, Victoria Falls (between Zambia and Zimbabwe) Iguassu Falls (between Brazil and Argentina,) the Great Barrier Reef, the Galapagos Archipelago, the Northern Lights (the Aurora Borealis) or the Fjords of Norway.

The Amazon Rainforest, the Perito Moreno Glacier, the Dome of the Rock, Israel, Salzburg, Austria Bora Bora, the Karnak Temple, Egypt. The Terracotta Warriors I China or Hong Kong Harbour or even the city of Mecca.

You could go on a pilgrimage to Santiago de Compostela. Visit the Leaning Tower of Pisa, the Eiffel Tower or the Panama Canal. Plan to visit all 7 continents or even visit every country in the world. You could plan to live in a foreign country for six months. Or visit a tropical island like Antigua, Barbados, Grenada or Tobago.

You could plan a trip to some of the most amazing buildings in the world like the Basilica di San Marco in Venice, St. Peter's Basilica in the Vatican, the Acropolis in Greece, the Alhambra in Spain. Gaudi's La Sagrada Familia in Barcelona, The Statues of Easter Island, Chile, the Kremlin in Moscow, the Pyramids of Giza,

Egypt. Stonehenge, United Kingdom, the Sydney Opera House,. Big Ben and the Houses of Parliament, London, the Parthenon in Greece, the Coliseum in Rome. Petra, Jordan, Christ the Redeemer, Brazil, the Great Wall of China, Chichen Itza, Mexico, the Taj Mahal, India or Notre Dame Cathedral, Paris .

If you are interest in art then some of the museums you could put on your list include El Prado in Madrid, the Uffizi Gallery in Florence, the Hermitage in St. Petersburg, Russia, Musée de l'Orangerie or the Louvre in Paris, the Metropolitan Museum of Art in New York, the British Museum or the Tate Gallery in London, the Van Gogh Museum, Amsterdam, the Egyptian Museum in Cairo, the Art Institute of Chicago or the Smithsonian Institute in Washington, DC.

You could plan a trip across America to see the Golden Gate Bridge in San Francisco, the Pike Place Market in Seattle, Mount Rushmore or Universal Studios, in Hollywood, California. You could visit the Empire State Building, climb up the Statue of Liberty, go to Faneuil Hall Marketplace, Boston or visit SeaWorld or Disney World in Orlando. You could visit Waikiki Beach, Oahu, Hawaii, or just visit all Fifty of the United States

If there is something you wish you had done as a child now is the time to add it to your list or learn as a hobby. You could learn how to use a pogo stick. You could learn to play chess, poker (or bridge) or pool. You could take up photography or learn to make pottery or to sculpt. You could take up astronomy, learn astrology or learn how to perform magic tricks. Keep bees. Learn to juggle.

Solve the Rubik's Cube. Build a village around a model train layout. Construct furniture. Do woodworking. Make stained glass windows. Learn to make candles. Make models of cars, ships or airplanes or build doll houses. Learn to brew beer. Take up gourmet cooking. Paint – watercolors, oil, acrylics. Take up gardening. Grow prize-winning roses. Restore a classic car. Restore antiques. Learn to draw. Become a Wine Connoisseur or a Cheese Connoisseur.

If you like to read why not make a list of 100 books you want to read. Read the complete works of Shakespeare. Read every novel that has won a Pulitzer Prize in the Fiction Category. Read all of the Russian classics. Read every book your favourite author has written. Read all of Agatha Christie's mystery novels.

If you are a movie buff, why not make a list of 100 movies you want to watch. Watch the American Film Institute's (AFI) 100 Funniest Movies. Watch the 10 greatest American movies of all time (as ranked by the AFI). Watch every movie that has won an Academy Award for Best Picture. Watch every movie that has won the Cannes Film Festival's Palme d'Or.

If none of the above are your thing then just have a happiness project. Start to release negative emotions and limiting beliefs. Start to allow yourself to make mistakes. discover your life's purpose. Learn not to take what others do or say personally. Figure out your priorities. Learn to act within your sphere of influence and stop worrying about things which are not within your control.

Become an early riser. Kick negative habits (smoking, overeating, watching too much television, and so on.) Attend one of Anthony Robbins' weekend events. Go to one of Steve Pavlina's Weekend Workshops in Las Vegas. Become a better public speaker by joining Toastmasters. Learn to say 'no' without feeling guilty.

You could educate yourself more by going back to finish school, get a college degree, get a Masters, get a PhD. Get into Medical School or get Certified as a Public Accountant. You could get an MBA or get Certified as a Financial Planner. Get into Harvard or get into Juilliard Shool of Music.

For those who you are who so inspired at this stage and are now ready to Hit the Big Time Bucket List. Here are some ideas for your remaining 29,000 days and big goals that you can aim for.

You could be interviewed by Oprah, be Time Magazine's Person of the Year, be interviewed by Piers Morgan.

Be listed as one of People Magazine's '50 Most Beautiful People'. Be on the cover of *Rolling Stone* Magazine. Have a street named after you. You could aim to be one of CNN's Heroes (CNN's global search for everyday people changing the world). Win a Nobel Prize. Receive a knighthood (or a damehood) from the Queen Elizabeth. Be elected to political office. Be inducted into a Hall of Fame. Be awarded a star on the Hollywood Walk of Fame. Cut the ribbon at a major opening. Win an Emmy. Make the front page of the newspaper. Be interviewed on The Today Show.

If you are more humble person you could aim to just make a difference in at least one person's life.

Build a Habitat for Humanity Home or volunteer at a soup

kitchen. Join the Peace Corps. If you have money then donate to a charity of your choice (anonymously or not). Make loans to entrepreneurs in developing countries. Join a Big Brother or a Big Sister Program. Volunteer at a Homeless Shelter. Donate blood. Donate clothes you no longer use to a battered women's shelter. Donate children's books to a hospital near your home. Mentor someone at work.

If you have always wanted to write then you could aim to get an article published in The New Yorker magazine or an article published in The Huffington Post. Write and publish a novel. Write a Number 1 New York Times Best Seller. Write an eBook. Write a children's book. Write a cookbook. Write a play. Write a travel book. Write a textbook. Publish a book of poetry. Write for a TV sitcom. Write a comic book. Crack the Top 100 on Amazon Kindle. Earn enough from your writing to be able to quit your day job.

If you want to be a performer, then audition for Britain's Got Talent or America's Got Talent, or for a role in a movie, a Broadway play or a TV sitcom. Apply to The Apprentice, or to be an extra in a film. You could be the lead role in your community theatre's next play or be in a commercial or a rock band.

If you want to try the high life before you kick the bucket then try to shop at Harrods. Charter a yacht. Own a beach house. Own a private jet. Spend some time in Martha's Vineyard. Spend a week at a 5-star spa. Shop in Rodeo Drive. Go to an auction at Christie's or Sotheby's Have "High Tea" at the Plaza Hotel in New York. Own a Rolls Royce, an Aston Martin, or a Bentley. Become an art collector.

Gamble at Monte Carlo and drive a Lamborghini or a Ferrari. Sleep in a castle or own an island.

What about ideas for your career, could you be recognised as an authority in your field. Be a world-renowned expert in your field. Be the best in the world in your field. Leave a valuable contribution in your area of expertise. Start your own business. Own a bar. Own a spa. Invent something. Invent a board game. Make a documentary film. Have your paintings exhibited in a gallery. Become a wild life photographer. Sell your original artwork. Become an interior designer. Become an architect. Design furniture. Be a clothes designer. Become a famous chef and open your own restaurant. Become a life coach. Become mayor of your city. Become a senator, a judge, a doctor, a nurse, a personal trainer, a yoga instructor, a coach, athlete, an A-list actor, a journalist, a newscaster, a teacher or a college professor.

Do you know how to use the internet to make money. Could you start a blog (have it get to the Technorati top 1000), create a YouTube video, become a Giant Squid on Squidoo or be highly influential on Social Media. Maybe you could make a five-figure income from your online ventures.

When it comes to money could you set goals and learn to become financially literate. Create a financial strategy. Invest in the stock market. Create enough passive income so that you don't have to work another day in your life. Create a trust fund for your child. Create a corporation to protect your assets or even open a Swiss bank account.

Do you want to improve your family relationships or find

the love of your life. Do you want to get married? Go on that honeymoon that keeps getting postponed. Have a child. Raise a happy and healthy child. Adopt a child. Create a home with an inviting, joyous, comfortable, loving atmosphere. Have a pet. Pass on a family heirloom to your child. Create a coat of arms for your family. Write a letter to each of your children telling them what you want them to know about your life and the lessons you've learned.

Do you want to do something crazy or odd before you die like run with the bulls. Or watch turtles hatch and run for the ocean. Have an aquarium. Swim with dolphins. Go whale-watching. See penguins in their natural habitat. See a platypus. See a koala. Visit the San Diego Zoo. Go on safari.

Save a species from extinction. Become a vegetarian. Adopt a pet from the animal shelter.

Milk a cow. Ride a camel in the Sahara desert. See gorillas in the wild in Uganda. Go bird watching in Costa Rica.

Do you need to become more spiritual during your remaining 29,000 days? Do you want to meet the Dalai Lama and/ or the Pope? Visit Tibet. Spend a week at a Silent Retreat. Experience bliss and find inner peace. Learn to forgive. Do all the lessons in 'A Course in Miracles'. Attend a Native American Sweat Lodge Ceremony. Become a Reiki Master. Heal your past. Learn to live in the now Take up yoga. Take up tai chi. Take up Qigong. Have a past life regression. Learn to meditate or go on an inner awakening retreat in India.

Is there something you have always wanted to see, well now

is your chance to write it down. How about seeing an opera at La Scala in Milan, an Armani fashion show or a concert by your favourite entertainer? Go to Carnegie Hall or see a Broadway Play. View a session of the US Supreme Court Go to a TED Talk. Go to the Super Bowl, the Olympics or the World Cup. Visit Wimbledon or the Kentucky Derby. Go To All Four Major Golf Tournaments: Masters, US Open, British Open and PGA Championship.

You could even add some foods you have never tasted to your list like trying Oysters, Gumbo, Chicken Tikka Masala, Churros, Caviar, Escargot, Truffle, or sample crab cakes in Baltimore, MD. Eat fugu (puffer fish from Japan) or try real balsamic vinegar (from Modena or Reggio Emilia in Italy).

You can do whatever you like, take what you want from this list or make up your own. You are alive and have freedom to do whatever you like. Remember he/ she who says something can't be done is usually interrupted by someone else doing it.

Life is a journey of 1,000 steps. The days are counting down, don't let one more pass you by without making that list or that plan. Remember to always jump and build your wings on the way down. There is never the right time, right place or right person around. Just do it now and overcome the fear. It is the fear which stops men and women being great. It's time to jump, so do it now.

Chapter 12

Get some Inspiration

I have collected many quotes over the years. Spend some time reading these great words from great people who have come before you. Hopefully they will inspire you as much as they have inspired me.

Go back a little to leap further.
(John Clarke)

It is hard to fail, but it is worse never to have tried to succeed.
(Theodore Roosevelt)

Half of the failures in life come from pulling one's horse when he is leaping.
(Thomas Hood)

I failed my way to success.
(Thomas Edison)

Our doubts are traitors, and make us lose the good we oft might win, by fearing to attempt.
(William Shakespeare)

Every failure brings with it the seed of an equivalent success.
(Napoleon Hill)

Failure is blindness to the strategic element in events; success is readiness for instant action when the opportune moment arrives.
(Newell D. Hillis)

They fail, and they alone, who have not striven.
(Thomas Bailey Aldrich)

We learn wisdom from failure much more than success. We often discover what we will do, by finding out what we will not do.
(Samuel Smiles)

I was never afraid of failure, for I would sooner fail than not be among the best.
(John Keats)

He that is down needs fear no fall.
(John Bunyan)

Never let the fear of striking out get in your way.
(George Herman "Babe" Ruth)

One who fears failure limits his activities. Failure is only the opportunity to more intelligently begin again.
(Henry Ford)

The greatest mistake you can make in life is to continually be afraid you will make one.
(Elbert Hubbard)

Failure is a trickster with a keen sense of irony and cunning. It takes great delight in tripping one when success is almost within reach.
(Napoleon Hill)

Little minds are tamed and subdued by misfortunes; but great minds rise above them.
(Washington Irving)

Our greatest glory consists not in never falling, but in rising every time we fall.
(Oliver Goldsmith)

Wherever we look upon this earth, the opportunities take shape within the problems.
(Nelson A. Rockefeller)

What would life be if we had no courage to attempt anything?
(Vincent Van Gogh)

The greatest men sometimes overshoot themselves, but then their very mistakes are so many lessons of instruction.
(Tom Browne)

Experience teaches slowly, and at the cost of mistakes.
(James A. Froude)

It is the want of diligence, rather than the want of means, that causes most failures.
(Alfred Mercier)

A man's life is interesting primarily when he has failed. I well know. For it's a sign that he tried to surpass himself.
(Georges Clemenceau)

He who fears being conquered is sure of defeat.
(Napoleon Bonaparte)

There is no failure except in no longer trying.
(Elbert Hubbard)

There is no impossibility to him who stands prepared to conquer every hazard. The fearful are the failing.
(Sarah J. Hale)

Disappointments are to the soul what thunderstorms are to the air.
(Johann C. F. Von Schiller)

Failure teaches success.
(Japanese Saying)

I have spread my dreams beneath your feet. Tread softly because you tread on my dreams.
(W.B. Yeats)

Go confidently in the direction of your dreams. Live the life you have imagined.
(Henry David Thoreau)

Every great dream begins with a dreamer. Always remember, you have within you the strength, the patience, and the passion to reach for the stars to change the world.
(Harriet Tubman)

Reach high, for stars lie hidden in your soul. Dream deep, for every dream precedes the goal.
(Pamela Vaull Starr)

All men dream but not equally. Those who dream by night in the dusty recesses of their minds wake in the day to find that it was vanity; but the dreamers of the day are dangerous men, for they may act their dream with open eyes to make it possible.
(T.E. Lawrence)

Our truest life is when we are in dreams awake.
(Henry David Thoreau)

So often times it happens that we live our lives in chains and we never even know we have the key.
(The Eagles)

The end of wisdom is to dream high enough not to lose the dream in the seeking of it.
(William Faulkner)

I like the dreams of the future better than the history of the past.
(Patrick Henry)

Hold fast to dreams, for if dreams die, life is a broken winged bird that cannot fly.
(Lanston Hughes)

You cannot dream yourself into a character: you must hammer and forge yourself into one.
(Henry D. Thoreau)

The future belongs to those who believe in the beauty of their dreams.
(Eleanor Roosevelt)

Commitment leads to action. Action brings your dream closer.
(Marcia Wieder)

Dreams are the touchstones of our character.
(Henry David Thoreau)

The question for each man to settle is not what he would do if he had means, time, influence and educational advantages; the question is what he will do with the things he has. The moment a young man ceases to dream or to bemoan his lack of opportunities and resolutely looks his conditions in the face, and resolves to change them, he lays the corner-stone of a solid and honourable success.
(Hamilton Wright Mabie)

The best way to make your dreams come true is to wake up.
(Paul Valery)

A skilful man reads his dreams for self-knowledge, yet not the details but the quality.
(Ralph Waldo Emerson)

Our waking hours form the text of our lives, our dreams, the commentary.
(Anonymous)

Hope is the dream of the waking man.
(French Proverb)

We are what we repeatedly do. Excellence, therefore, is not an act but a habit.
(Aristotle)

Take calculated risks. That is quite different from being rash.
(George S. Patton)

Storms make oaks take roots.
(Proverb)

If you do not hope, you will not find what is beyond your hopes.
(St. Clement of Alexandra)

We are all inventors, each sailing out on a voyage of discovery, guided each by a private chart, of which there is no duplicate. The world is all gates, all opportunities.
(Ralph Waldo Emerson)

Seek the lofty by reading, hearing and seeing great work at some moment every day.
(Thornton Wilder)

The only way of finding the limits of the possible is by going beyond them into the impossible.
(Arthur C. Clarke)

Without inspiration the best powers of the mind remain dormant. There is a fuel in us which needs to be ignited with sparks.
(Johann Gottfried Von Herder)

Hope is like the sun, which, as we journey toward it, casts the shadow of our burden behind us.
(Samuel Smiles)

Work spares us from three evils: boredom, vice, and need.
(Voltaire)

If the wind will not serve, take to the oars.
(Latin Proverb)

Men's best successes come after their disappointments.
(Henry Ward Beecher)

You cannot plough a field by turning it over in your mind.
(Author Unknown)

The best way out is always through.
(Robert Frost)

Do not wait to strike till the iron is hot; but make it hot by striking.
(William B. Sprague)

Nothing will ever be attempted if all possible objections must first be overcome.
(Samuel Johnson)

Fortune favours the brave.
(Publius Terence)

When the best things are not possible, the best may be made of those that are.
(Richard Hooker)

He who hesitates is lost.
(Proverb)

If you want to succeed in the world, you must make your own opportunities as you go on. The man who waits for some seventh wave to toss him on dry land will find that the seventh wave is a long time coming. You can commit no greater folly than to sit by the roadside until someone comes along and invites you to ride with him to wealth or influence.
(John B. Gough)

Great spirits have always encountered violent opposition from mediocre minds.
(Albert Einstein)

Believe with all of your heart that you will do what you were made to do.
(Orison Swett Marden)

Knowing is not enough; we must apply. Willing is not enough; we must do.
(Johann Wolfgang von Goethe)

We are still masters of our fate. We are still captains of our souls.
(Winston Churchill)

Nothing great was ever achieved without enthusiasm.
(Ralph Waldo Emerson)

Reach perfection.
(Baltasar Gracián)

For hope is but the dream of those that wake.
(Matthew Prior)

Constant dripping hollows out a stone.
(Lucretius)

Nothing contributes so much to tranquilize the mind as a steady purpose a point on which the soul may fix its intellectual eye.
(Mary Shelley)

Try not to become a man of success but a man of value.
(Albert Einstein)

If you have built castles in the air, your work need not be lost; that is where they should be. Now put foundations under them.
(Henry David Thoreau)

Inspiration and genius, one and the same.
(Victor Hugo)

If you would create something, you must be something.
(Johann Wolfgang von Goethe)

Every artist was first an amateur.
(Ralph Waldo Emerson)

The more difficulties one has to encounter, within and without, the more significant and the higher in inspiration his life will be.
(Horace Bushnell)

Life has no smooth road for any of us; and in the bracing atmosphere of a high aim the very roughness stimulates the climber to steadier steps, till the legend, over steep ways to the stars, fulfils itself.
(W. C. Doane)

Experience is the child of thought, and thought is the child of action.
(Benjamin Disraeli)

Do we not all agree to call rapid thought and noble impulse by the name of inspiration?
(George Eliot)

No great man ever complains of want of opportunities.
(Ralph Waldo Emerson)

Men do less than they ought, unless they do all they can.
(Thomas Carlyle)

Let thy words be few. Happy are those who dream dreams and are ready to pay the price to make them come true.
(Leon J. Suenes)

The power of imagination makes us infinite.
(John Muir)

First say to yourself what you would be; and then do what you have to do.
(Epictetus)

Along with success comes a reputation for wisdom.
(Euripides)

They can because they think they can.
(Virgil)

Nothing can stop the man with the right mental attitude from achieving his goal; nothing on earth can help the man with the wrong mental attitude.
(Thomas Jefferson)

Keep steadily before you the fact that all true success depends at last upon yourself.
(Theodore T. Hunger)

We are all motivated by a keen desire for praise, and the better a man is, the more he is inspired to glory.
(Cicero)

The thing always happens that you really believe in; and the belief in a thing makes it happen.
(Frank Lloyd Wright)

The surest way not to fail is to determine to succeed.
(Richard Sheridan)

A failure is a man who has blundered, but is not able to cash in on the experience.
(Elbert Hubbard)

There is only one success - to be able to spend your life in your own way.
(Christopher Morley)

Success is sweet: the sweeter if long delayed and attained through manifold struggles and defeats.
(A. Branson Alcott)

The secret of success is to know something nobody else knows.
(Aristotle Onassis)

The greatest results in life are usually attained by simple means and the exercise of ordinary qualities. These may for the most part be summed in these two: common-sense and perseverance.
(Owen Feltham)

The difference between a successful person and others is not a lack of strength, not a lack of knowledge, but rather a lack of will.
(Vince Lombardi)

Everyone has a fair turn to be as great as he pleases.
(Jeremy Collier)

I cannot give you the formula for success, but I can give you the formula for failure, which is: tlry to please everybody.
(Herbert Bayard Swope)

Success does not consist in never making blunders, but in never making the same one a second time.
(Josh Billings)

The secret of success in life is for a man to be ready for his opportunity when it comes.
(Earl of Beaconsfield)

Success is the good fortune that comes from aspiration, desperation, perspiration and inspiration.
(Evan Esar)

If you wish success in life, make perseverance your bosom friend, experience your wise counselor, caution your elder brother, and hope your guardian genius.
(Joseph Addison)

Impatience never commanded success.
(Edwin H. Chapin)

The talent of success is nothing more than doing what you can do, well.
(Henry W. Longfellow)

To climb steep hills requires a slow pace at first.
(William Shakespeare)

Try not to become a man of success but a man of value.
(Albert Einstein)

The man who makes a success of an important venture never wails for the crowd. He strikes out for himself. It takes nerve, it takes a great lot of grit; but the man that succeeds has both. Anyone can fail. The public admires the man who has enough confidence in himself to take a chance. These chances are the main things after all. The man who tries to succeed must expect to be criticised. Nothing important was ever done but the greater number consulted previously doubted the possibility. Success is the accomplishment of that which most people think can't be done.
(C. V. White)

If at first you don't succeed, try, try again. Then quit. There's no use being a damn fool about it.
(W.C. Fields)

Success is the sum of small efforts, repeated day in and day out.
(Robert Collier)

The ability to convert ideas to things is the secret to outward success.
(Henry Ward Beecher)

The ability to concentrate and to use your time well is everything if you want to succeed in business or almost anywhere else for that matter.
(Lee Iacocca)

A wise man will make more opportunities than he finds.
(Francis Bacon)

In everything the ends well defined are the secret of durable success.
(Victor Cousins)

Winning isn't everything, but wanting to win is.
(Vince Lombardi)

Failures do what is tension relieving, while winners do what is goal achieving.
(Dennis Waitley)

Goals are the fuel in the furnace of achievement.
(Brian Tracy)

The great and glorious masterpiece of man is to know how to live to purpose.
(Michel de Montaigne)

Ah, but a man's reach should exceed his grasp, or what's a heaven for?
(Robert Browning)

The significance of a man is not in what he attains but in what he longs to attain.
(Kahlil Gibran)

Every ceiling, when reached, becomes a floor, upon which one walks as a matter of course and prescriptive right.
(Aldous Huxley)

If you don't know where you are going, you'll end up someplace else.
(Yogi Berra)

Life can be pulled by goals just as surely as it can be pushed by drives.
(Viktor Frankl)

The virtue lies in the struggle, not in the prize.
(Richard Monckton Milnes)

There is no happiness except in the realization that we have accomplished something.
(Henry Ford)

Our plans miscarry because they have no aim. When a man does not know what harbour he is making for, no wind is the right wind.
(Seneca)

It is not enough to take steps which may some day lead to a goal; each step must be itself a goal and a step likewise.
(Johann Wolfgang Von Goethe)

Who aims at excellence will be above mediocrity; who aims at mediocrity will be far short of it.
(Burmese Saying)

In the absence of clearly defined goals, we become strangely loyal to performing daily acts of trivia.
(Author Unknown)

Don't bunt. Aim out of the ballpark.
(David Ogilvy)

There are two things to aim at in life; first to get what you want, and after that to enjoy it. Only the wisest of mankind has achieved the second.
(Logan Pearsall Smith)